Anonymous

Reunion of the Dickinson family

At Amherst, Mass., August 8th and 9th, 1883 - Vol. 1

Anonymous

Reunion of the Dickinson family
At Amherst, Mass., August 8th and 9th, 1883 - Vol. 1

ISBN/EAN: 9783337732141

Printed in Europe, USA, Canada, Australia, Japan

Cover: Foto ©ninafisch / pixelio.de

More available books at **www.hansebooks.com**

OF THE

DICKINSON FAMILY,

AT

AMHERST, MASS.,

August 8th and 9th, 1883.

WITH APPENDIX.

BINGHAMTON PUBLISHING COMPANY.
1884.

DICKINSON
FAMILY.

Amherst, Mass.

Aug. 8-9, 1883.

ESSE QUAM VIDERI.

	PAGE
Introduction	1
Roll of Honor	5
Voices of the Past	9
Opening Prayer	10
President's Address	13
Hymn by Mrs. Currier	20
Historical Address	21
Hymn by Alice E. Dickinson	50
Poem by Mrs. Elizabeth D. Currier	50
Essay by Edward B. Dickinson	62
Poem by Gideon Dickinson, M. D	77
Address of Dr. Hiram Corson	94
" Wharton Dickinson	95
" George Montague	105
" John W. Dickinson	109
Letter from Don M. Dickinson	115
" Daniel H. Wells	117
Address of Hon. Wm. F. Dickinson	120
" Wm. L. Dickinson	121
" George H. Corson	124
Letter from A. D. Dickinson	127
" Wm. J. Dickenson	128
" Alexander White	129

	PAGE
Address of Stillman B. Pratt	131
" E. N. Dickinson	133
" Asa W. Dickinson	134
Letter from Dr. Wm. Dickinson	136
Hymn by Mary E. Bullard	138
Letter from Rev. Wm. C. Dickinson	139
" Henry W. Tafft	140
" Charles Dickinson Adams	141
Hymn by Gideon Dickinson, M. D.	144
Song by Chas. M. Dickinson	145
Proceedings of August 9th	147

APPENDIX MATTER.

Sketch of Nathaniel Dickinson	153
Branches from Symon Dickenson	154
Genealogical Chart	160
Will of Sir Gilbert Grafton	161
Sketch of Daniel S. Dickinson	163
" Mahlon Dickerson	166
" Gov. Philemon Dickerson	167
" Jonathan Dickinson	167
" Samuel Dickinson	168
" Timothy Dickinson	168
" John Dickinson	170
" Samuel Fowler Dickinson	172
" Austin Dickinson	174
" Baxter Dickinson, D. D.	176
" Gen. Philemon Dickinson	178
Letter from Daniel Webster	179
Sketch of Dr. Edmund Dickenson	180
" Anson Dickinson	180

	PAGE
Letter from Washington Irving	182
"The Children," by Chas. M. Dickinson	183
Hymn to the Trinity, by Rev. L. R. Dickinson	186
Sketch of Edward Dickinson	188
" Nathan Dickinson	189
Proposed Family History	191
Sketch of Wm. L. Dickinson	201
" Andrew Dickinson	202
" Juliette Dickinson	203
" Emma A. Dickinson	203
" Mary E. Dickinson	204

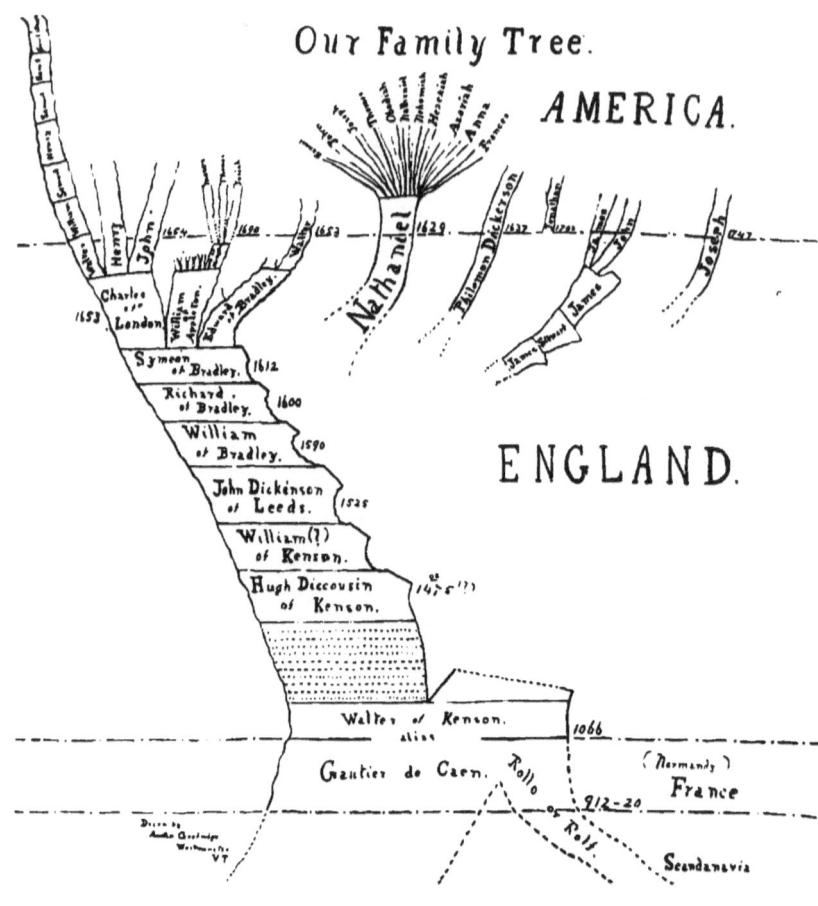

INTRODUCTORY.

———0———

As the late reunion of the Dickinson Family has become an historical event, to which many will refer as an occasion of much enjoyment, it is proper that a relation should be made of the manner by which so much interest was concentrated, and so large an assembly was convened.

One who traces his lineal descent from the first Nathaniel Dickinson, of Hadley, and early inspired with a great respect for the name, [whose grandfather and his sons lived and acted in the times which tried men's souls,] had cherished a desire to see called together the widely separated members of the family.

He knew that to accomplish this object, some *one* must act, and believing that the proposal of a general meeting would receive a general indorsement, he decided to take the responsibility of calling the attention of the great family to its consideration.

His first movement was naturally among those nearest to him,—the worthy agricultural class of his native town of Amherst, quite numerously bearing the name, all of whom cordially responded in favor of the meeting.

Then letters followed to M. F. Dickinson, Jr., Esq., of Boston; John W. Dickinson, of Boston, Secretary of the State Board of Education; Rev. Chas. A. Dickinson, of Lowell, and Austin Goodridge, Esq., of Westminster, Vt. From all of these able and influential gentlemen was received enthusiastic approval of the proposed meeting, and expressions of willingness to aid in making it a decided success.

The Dickinsons from Worcester, Springfield, Northampton and Hadley responded with the like spirit of approval. The names on the list of committee had increased, and Mr. F. W. Dickinson, of Springfield, had accepted the office of Secretary, and was devoting his untiring efforts to disseminate notices of the proposed meeting, and was receiving almost unanimous expressions favorable to the desired object.

All this preliminary progress had been made in the two months ending December 15th, 1882. Letters were received from distinguished Dickinsons from Connecticut, New York and Pennsylvania—from the West and South, with hearty approval. Even our Brothers, representing the Society of Friends, cordially responded, and it seemed that information of the meeting had reached the remotest section inhabited by a Dickinson, and all seemed moved with a common desire to participate in the proposed reunion.

With so great encouragement the committee proceeded early in the year '83 to issue the following formal call:

"MEETING OF THE DICKINSON FAMILY."

A MEETING OF THE DICKINSON FAMILY, INCLUDING DESCENDANTS IN THE FEMALE LINE, WILL BE HELD IN AMHERST, MASSACHUSETTS, ON WEDNESDAY, AUGUST 8, 1883, AT TEN O'CLOCK, A. M.

ALL ARE CORDIALLY INVITED TO ATTEND.

The objects of the meeting are to commemorate the 223d anniversary of the settlement in Hadley, Mass., of

Nathaniel Dickinson, who was the ancestor of the New England branch of the family, and to testify our high veneration for an ancestry worthy of a descent so large in number, and so honorable in character; to make more intimate acquaintance with each other, to cultivate more fully those higher attributes of our nature which have their source in the love of kindred, to recall from forgetfulness the history of the labors, trials and successes of our fathers, and by appropriate record render their names imperishable.

Addresses and other interesting exercises appropriate to the occasion may be expected.

It is desirable that all branches of the widely extended family should be represented at the meeting, especially those bearing the name of Dickinson among the Society of Friends, as probably all of the name of Dickinson have a common origin, which it is hoped will be traced at this meeting. All are kindly urged to be present, and all will receive a cordial welcome.

Those who receive this notice are requested to extend it as widely as possible, and also to bring with them to the meeting any portraits, relicts or mementos which may illustrate the past history of any of the name of Dickinson. It is expected that the meeting will develop such interest and information concerning the family as will lead to the early preparation and publication of a general genealogical history. An early reply addressed to the Secretary is requested, which it is hoped may contain congratulations and a promise of attendance. To all who reply, a program of the exercises will be sent when published. All inquiries will receive due attention."

The names of fifty-seven members of the general committee were appended to the above call.

The important work of preparing the order of exercises

next claimed the attention of the committee, and upon this labor, as in the past, the requirements of the meeting were fully met. M. F. Dickinson, Jr., Esq., of Boston, consented to act as President, and to give the address of welcome, and Rev. Chas. A. Dickinson, of Lowell, agreed to prepare the historical address; and for their generous labors in redeeming from the obscurity of past ages so much of interest concerning the name, the Dickinsons will hold them in perpetual remembrance.

Other gentlemen and ladies, in response to the request of the Secretary, contributed interesting addresses, poems and hymns. Mr. Levi E. Dickinson, of North Amherst, led the choir and the united voices of the large audience in those sweet songs—the melody of which is yet vibrating in many hearts.

The order of exercises was completed and issued early in July. The contract for dinners for 400 persons was guaranteed. Among the minor preparations was that of the

DECORATION OF THE STAGE.

In the rear of the Speaker's desk, upon a frame eighteen feet high and ten feet wide, was a tasteful ornamentation, consisting of a background of various colored bunting, surmounted by a shield and flags, with laurel wreaths and festoons, (wrought by the willing hands of several Dickinson young ladies), in the centre of which was suspended a terra cotta colored scroll, prepared by Mr. George Montague, on which was emblazoned in golden letters, the names of distinguished Dickinsons, as follows:

ROLL OF HONOR.

NATHANIEL DICKINSON.
GOV. JOHN DICKINSON, LL.D.
HON. DANIEL S. DICKINSON.
DR. EDMUND DICKENSON.
GEN. PHILEMON DICKINSON.
GOV. MAHLON DICKERSON.
GOV. PHILEMON DICKERSON.
PRESIDENT JONATHAN DICKINSON.
REV. TIMOTHY DICKINSON.
REV. BAXTER DICKINSON, D. D.
HON. SAMUEL FOWLER DICKINSON.
HON. EDWARD DICKINSON.
REV. AUSTIN DICKINSON.
ANSON DICKINSON, (the Artist.)

An historical chart hung next to the Roll of Honor—the work of Austin Goodridge, of Vermont—showing the Norman and English origin of the family, and exhibiting the several branches of the family, from Symon Dickenson, of Bradley, to the present generation.

On the right of the Roll of Honor hung the portrait of John Dickinson; on the left, and beneath, two of Daniel S. Dickinson. On either side of these were two other portraits, and below were seen that of Nathan Dickinson, formerly of Amherst, (Additional Notes) and a photograph of Judge Asa Dickinson, of Springfield, Prince Edward County, Virginia. Beside these were views of the first house in Amherst, built by a Dickinson, and, resting from its labors, against the wall, the musket of one of Nathaniel's sons, used in killing Indians and wolves.

The arrangement of the stage was under the direction of Mr. George Montague, and to his tasteful and energetic supervision, and to the ladies of the family, as well as to the efficient Secretary, Mr. Francke W. Dickinson, and the Recording Secretary, Edward B. Dickinson, who prepared and furnished a very full and correct stenographic report of the proceedings—to all these, lasting obligations are due.

The day was most propitious. Classic Amherst, dreaming through her Summer siesta, was thronged with strangers, of not unfamiliar countenance. The coaches were loaded down, and greetings of kinsmen long separated were heard from stage-top and in corridor. In the streets "there was hurrying to and fro," and "all went merry as a marriage bell." A distinguished member of the family, on inquiring for his room at the Amherst House, was asked, "What is your name?" "Dickinson," he replied. He might as well have said, "N. or M.," for said mine host, "'Dickinson!' There are six hundred of them, and some are in the woods." Persons addressing "Mr. Dickinson" were answered by a dozen voices at once. Never was such fallacy manifest as Shakespeare's "What's in a name?"

At ten o'clock the hall was thronged with a representative assembly from fifteen States. All the family wore upon the left breast a green silk ribbon, on which was stamped in gold the family arms, viz.: On a green shield a gold cross between four hinds' heads. The crest, a hind's head; the motto, *Esse Quam Videri*—"To be, rather than to appear." On the stage were the officers of the day; while, as if overshadowing the hushed assemblage, the presence of the mighty dead filled all the room with solemnity. The words spoken and the thoughts inspired by that day will not die, but will move the whole of this great household in years to come, to do honor to that "good name which is better than great riches."

On the second day of this "feast of ingathering," a goodly number of the company enjoyed a trip to Old Hadley and to Mt. Holyoke. We drove "Tally-ho" through the broad street of Hadley. Certainly, the forefathers who laid out this magnificent avenue could not have been "narrow-minded." It is about 200 feet wide ; down the middle is a grass-plot 100 feet wide and one mile long, flanked on each side by a roadway of 25 feet, and on the outside of the roadways by another green sward and walk of 25 feet. The edges of the main grass-plot and also of the walks are overshadowed by double rows of elms. We visited the old graveyard of Hadley and read the inscriptions, one of the oldest being that of Nathaniel Dickinson, who died in his eightieth year. We also stopped to drink from the old well on the site of the Dickinson homestead, and thence proceeded to Mt. Holyoke, dining together, and enjoying the glorious landscapes of the Connecticut Valley. Returning to Amherst, some of us paid our respects to certain venerable gods of Assyria in the college museum. Had these been less hideous, we might have fancied them to be some of our Puritan fathers, looking down upon our frivolity, with austere reproach.

So ended the first, but not, we all believe, the last reunion of the Dickinsons.

THE PROCEEDINGS.

College Hall, Amherst,
August 8, 1883, 10 o'clock A. M.

The President, M. F. Dickinson, Jr., Esq., called the meeting to order in the following words:

LADIES AND GENTLEMEN: I have been requested to call this meeting to order; and I invite Mr. F. W. Dickinson, of Springfield, Mass., who has acted as the official Secretary of this committee, to announce the officers of the day.

Mr. F. W. Dickinson then announced the list of officers of the organization as follows:

President—M. F. Dickinson, Jr.

Vice-Presidents—Dr. John F. Ely, Cedar Rapids, Iowa; Henry Woods, Boston, Mass.; Aug. N. Currier, Worcester, Mass.; Chas. F. Raymond, Cambridge, Mass.; Judge Wm. F. Dickinson, Aurora, Ill.; Wm. L. Dickinson, Jersey City, N. J.; Edward Dickinson, Laramie, W. T.; Daniel H. Dickinson, Hadley, Mass.; John W. Dickinson, Boston, Mass.; William Dickinson, Worcester, Mass.; Perez Dickinson, Knoxville, Tenn.; Elijah W. Dickinson, Springfield, Mass.; Marquis F. Dickinson, Amherst, Mass.; George R. Dickinson, Springfield, Mass.; Henry K. W. Dickinson, Northampton, Mass.; Elijah M. Dickinson, Fitchburg, Mass.; Gen. Leonard A. Dickinson, Hartford, Conn.; Franklin P. Dickinson, Hartford, Conn.; Austin Goodridge, Westminster, Vt.; William P. Dickinson, Chicago, Ill.; Edmund N. Dickinson, Amherst, Mass.; G. Fayette Dickinson, M. D., East Chatham, N. Y.; James W. Dickinson, Cleveland, Ohio; Julian G. Dickinson, Detroit, Mich.; Noah Dickinson, Amherst, Mass.; Frederick Dickinson, Billerica, Mass.; Pomeroy P. Dickinson, New York; Samuel D. Partridge, Milwaukee, Wis.; Levi E. Dickinson, North Amherst, Mass.; Henry W. Dickinson, San Francisco, Cal.; Charles Dickinson, New Britain, Conn.; George Montague, Amherst, Mass.

Secretary and Treasurer—Francke W. Dickinson, Springfield, Mass.

Recording Secretary—Edward B. Dickinson, New York.

The officers thus announced by the Secretary were unanimously elected to the offices for which they were respectively named.

The audience then joined in singing the first song on the program.

THE VOICES OF THE PAST.

Words by Gideon Dickinson, M. D., of Milford, Mass.,
Music by Charles B. Dickinson, of New York.

Drawn by the secret tie of kindred blood,
 From many a distant home, to-day, we come
To walk this vale, by yon fair river's flood,
 Where first our common sire did build a home.

And as we walked the shadowy streets, this morn,
 There rose strange phantoms from the distant past,
And down the corridors of time were borne,
 Echoes that thrilled the soul, like trumpet blast.

Oh, was it to my listening ear alone
 That voices from the past, this morning, came,
As, musingly, I wandered near the home
 Where first, within this land, arose our name?

Heard ye not voices in the sighing trees
  That waved above you as ye passed along?
Did not yon river, rolling to the seas,
  Murmur from the dark past a mystic song?

Did not strange voices whisper in each ear:—
  "Honor, to-day, the sire from whom ye sprang!
Ages ago he toiled and struggled here,
  Where forests wild with wilder war-whoops rang."

"Ages have rolled since with a patriot's care,
  He sought a wilderness to build a home,
And boldly brought his household gods, e'en where
  The savage red man and wild beasts did roam."

And are our souls, to-day, so cold and dead
  As not to thrill at mention of his name?
The west wind sighs above his lowly bed
  Where, by yon stream, he sleeps unknown to fame.

But this fair land and towering, stately domes
  Attest the worth and wisdom of his toil;
And proud descendants, in fair, happy homes,
  Inheriting his name, possess the soil.

Lives there among them all a soul so dead
  As not to love the soil whereon we stand?
That never, in his pride of heart, hath said,
  God bless our patriot sire and native land?

The President.—I will ask the audience to unite in prayer, which will be offered by the Rev. Legh Richmond Dickinson, Rector of Grace Church, Great Bend, Pennsylvania.

PRAYER.

O Lord God, there is no God like Thee in the Heaven or on the earth, who keepest covenant and showest mercy unto Thy servants, that walk before Thee with all their heart. The merciful goodness of the Lord endureth for ever and ever upon them that fear Him, and His righteousness upon children's children, even upon such as think upon His commandments to do them.

The merciful and gracious Lord hath so done His marvellous works that they ought to be had in remembrance. O God, we have heard with our ears, and our fathers have declared unto us, the noble works that Thou didst in their days, and in the old time before them.

We are assembled to commemorate Thy favor and goodness to us as a family. We thank Thee, that as Thou didst call Abraham, the father of the faithful, out of the land of his nativity into the land which Thou didst give to him and to his children, to be their inheritance, so Thou didst bring our ancestors out of the place of their forefathers into this good land and large, and didst give it to them and to their children, with others, to be their heritage for ever. O Lord God, we magnify Thy name for Thy goodness in vouchsafing to prepare for us such a goodly heritage. Thou broughtest our fathers through fire and water into a land of brooks of water, of fountains and depths, that spring out of valleys and hills.

What shall we render to the Lord for all His mercies to us and for all His dealings with those who have gone before us? We bless Thy name for Thy goodness manifested to Thy servants who have departed this life in peace and who now rest from their labors. We thank Thee that by Thy grace they were enabled to fulfill their part in life, more with a view of serving Thee than of magnifying or exalting themselves, and that in all the walks of life they proved themselves worthy of the trust committed to them. We thank Thee that Thou didst make them men and women of integrity and self-sacrifice, transmitting to their posterity the blessings prepared for them.

We pray Thee, O Lord God, that the example of our fathers, brought to our minds to-day, may be an incentive to us to act well our part in that state of life in which Thou hast been pleased to place us. Graciously do Thou strengthen us, O Lord, by these noble examples, to do worthily that which Thou givest us to do. Grant that Thy blessing may be upon this assemblage; may it encourage all who are gathered here, from the youngest to the oldest, to do, every one, his work with his might, so that we may hand down unimpaired the trust delivered to us, and be not ashamed of our part in the stewardship appointed us.

We pray Thee, O Lord, to be with us on this occasion. Grant that we may find it pleasant to meet together. May our children be animated by this opportunity which Thou hast given us of gathering together, to do better than we have done, through the privileges which shall be their inheritance and through the consciousness of the responsibility laid upon them.

And now, O Lord our God, let Thy mercy be upon us, even as we do put our trust in Thee. Show Thy servants Thy work, and their children Thy glory, that our sons may grow up as the young plants, and that our daughters may be as the polished corners of the temple. Multiply, Lord God, our posterity, as the sand of the sea shore and as the stars of heaven in multitude. We thank Thee for all Thy goodness to us in the past, and we humbly pray that Thou wilt be with us and help us to meet that which is to come to us in the future. And grant that at last, when the great day of reckoning shall call us together, we may all stand on the right hand of Him whom Thou hast appointed to be the Judge of the quick and the dead, and be admitted into those heavenly mansions where the redeemed of all ages meet, to part no more.

Hear us in our petitions, and help us to say, in Thy Name:

Our Father, who art in Heaven, hallowed be Thy Name. Thy kingdom come. Thy will be done on earth, as it is in Heaven. Give us this day our daily bread. And forgive us our trespasses, as we forgive those who trespass against us. And lead us not into temptation; but deliver us from evil: For Thine is the kingdom, and the power, and the glory, for ever and ever. Amen.

The President—The Chair will be obliged if the members of the Committee and the Vice-Presidents who have been named will take seats on the platform. Most of us are strangers to each other, and we desire to get better acquainted.

Such of the members of the Committee and the Vice-Presidents as were present, having taken their seats upon the platform, the President proceeded to deliver the following

ADDRESS OF WELCOME.

It is natural for all men to take pride in a worthy ancestry. There is a deep and pure satisfaction in contemplating the virtuous characters of our fathers, and in recalling the notable events with which they may have been identified. What peculiar charm lingers around the homes where they lived; what romantic interest attaches to the scenes amid which they moved; how reverently we tread soil in which they sleep!

This loyalty to the memory of our fathers is not dependent upon an ancestral record of distinguished public service; it is not conditioned upon the inheritance of great ancestral renown. The sentiment is instinctive; it appeals to the consciousness of all classes and conditions of men. It may, indeed, be carried so far as to degenerate into vulgar assumption; it sometimes offends us by its intolerant and intolerable conceit. Especially is this likely to be so where social distinctions are sharply defined, and where governments rest upon hereditary privileges. But the levelling tendencies of American society are such that the feeling of family pride is, perhaps, less obtrusive here than elsewhere. We have very little of inherited renown. No man among us expects to be lifted into positions of prominence upon the shoulders of his ancestors, nor to exert any lasting influence on their account. Yet, after all, it seems to be true that the instinct of ancestral pride, though less demonstrative, is no less general and genuine here than elsewhere.

It is therefore altogether natural and proper that the representatives of a numerous family should gather in this manner, to honor the worthy character of its earliest ancestors, to perpetuate the family traditions and history, to revisit the homestead of an important branch of the family, and to cement those ties of friendship and fellowship which should happily unite all who share a common descent and name.

Were this reunion in Virginia, the seat of a distinguished branch of the Dickinsons, the Cavalier of the seventeenth century might claim our especial notice. If we were gathered in New Jersey or Pennsylvania, where have shone some of the brightest names in our family annals, I might discourse of the soldiers and statesmen of the Revolutionary period. Here in Massachusetts such reflections as the place suggests to one who traces his lineage, through seven generations, from one of the pioneers of this ancient county of Hampshire, may not be entirely inappropriate.

How marvellous in its results was the movement which peopled New England. Where shall we look for the parallel of that emigration? It was short, lasting hardly more than twenty years. Beginning in 1620 it was substantially over in 1640. It was not in any sense a great popular movement. Its fortunes were not determined by its size. The number who came over was not large enough to make that by any means a chief element of its success. How insignificant in this regard, compared with the multitudes who have swelled the other great emigrations of the world, appear the twenty-five thousand Englishmen who, during that period, laid the foundations of New England.

But its lack of numbers was not the only apparent weakness of this movement. It enjoyed the patronage neither of wealth, nor of men in high social position, nor of political favorites. It was not a great commercial enterprise like all the other important English emigrations. It was not a movement born of national pride, eager to propagate its distinctive ideas and traits.. In its scheme robbery and conquest found no place. Its sword was never drawn save in self defence. It did not seek its own aggrandizement at the expense of weak and inoffensive nations. It turned no envious eye upon the treasures of ancient dynasties. It lifted no iron hand to enslave or murder whole races under the guise of religious zeal. It bore none of the aspects of aggressiveness. On the contrary, it seemed to lack all those elements of strength which have generally been thought requisite in founding states. Yet it is no exaggeration to say that the movement left an impress upon the human race which has been unsurpassed in history; and that none of the great emigrations, whether ancient or modern, ever contributed more largely to man's happiness and permanent welfare. And its distinctive character may be summed up in this statement, that it had its origin in pious hearts, that it found its highest sanctions in the separate conscience of each of its promoters, and that it had a high and single aim. Its success lay in the character, the motives, and the singleness of aim, of the men who em-

barked in it. They were not engaged in a mere struggle for civil rights and religious freedom. Their enterprise meant more than either, more than both, of these. Its object was the restoration of the theocracy—the founding of a Christian State. As Dr. Ellis has said, "Their lofty and soul enthralling aim   *   *   *   *
was the establishment and administration here of a religious and civil commonwealth which should have the same relation to the spirit and letter of the whole Bible that the Jewish commonwealth bore to the law of Moses." You may say that their dream was not realized, that their scheme was impracticable. They did indeed, fail to re-establish the theocracy. Still it stands as the irreversible verdict of history that it was the lofty ideal of the Pilgrim and the Puritan, which ensured to America the enjoyment of civil and religious liberty, an independent sovereignty, and a democratic form of government. Thank God for the men of one idea!

It is hard for us of to-day to realize what loyalty to this idea cost the men of 1620 and 1630. It involved self expatriation—leaving home forever. When the shores of England faded from sight they had taken their last look of all that contributes most largely to the comfort and happiness of life. Before them was the treacherous ocean, over whose weary leagues their crowded ships must toil through lengthening weeks and months. Awaiting them was an inhospitable shore, three thousand miles from the scenes they loved. On that rugged coast, or in the gloomy depths of the forests beyond, they were to live, and there they must die and be buried. And into these distant regions of toil, of privation, of insecurity, and of danger, they were bearing their scanty possessions and even their wives and little children. One hope, one only, brightened the uncertain future. God would watch over his people; their cause would surely be His care! In their dream of a Christian commonwealth they found both their incentive to labor and their solace in distress. Though unconscious, in a great degree, of the vast destinies involved in their enterprise, they were not unworthy of the high trusts with which they were charged. Neither cold, nor famine, nor pestilence, nor suffering of any kind, could loosen their hold upon the high purpose to which they had consecrated their lives. The voices of their detractors have long since been silenced. The greatest statesman and orator of America never found a theme more worthy of his powers than was afforded him at Plymouth on the two hundredth anniversary of the landing of the Pilgrims; while the most brilliant, and the most philosophical, of modern English historians have vied with each other in the ardor of their eulogiums upon the character, the motives, and the lasting influence, of the founders of New England.

It is no mean distinction to have descended from such stock. One of those adventurous spirits was the common ancestor of most of the five hundred people whom I see before me; the earliest one of whom, so far as I know, we, of the Massachusetts branch, have any certain knowledge.

It is now almost two hundred and fifty years since Nathaniel Dickinson (1) first appeared as a figure of some prominence in one of the remotest of the river settlements. Landing at Boston about 1630, he did not linger long at the Bay. From Watertown he plunged into the wilderness, and with his wife and four little children found a home, prior to 1637, at Wethersfield, forty or fifty miles below us. Cast out from thence, twenty years later, in one of those theological convulsions in which the period was prolific, he led his patriarchal household, then increased to nine sons and two or three daughters, up the Conecticut, into this fair and fruitful intervale which lies at our feet. Here, as one of the original settlers of Hadley, in 1659, he fixed the permanent seat of the

New England branch of our family, and deeply rooted the name of Dickinson; and here nine succeeding generations have already risen to call him blessed. He is said to have surveyed the lots which were apportioned among the settlers, and to have laid out the broad and stately "Middle Street" which, stretching across the peninsula a full mile, at a width of twenty rods, and including about forty acres within its boundaries, is so justly famous among the noteworthy objects of the valley. At the lower end of that street, on its east side, adjoining the "Bay Road," which there crosses it, he established the family homestead, the eastern portion of which, fortunately, has never passed from the possession of his descendants of the same name. There he lived, with the exception of a short residence across the river in Hatfield, until he died. He was a man of substance for those days, rating with the highest in the division of lands. He became a freeman of the Colony in 1661, was the first Town Recorder, twice a Selectman, often one of the "Raters," or Assessors, one of the "Commissioners," or Town Magistrates, and a Deacon of the Church throughout his life. His interest in education is attested by the fact that in 1667 he was chosen one of the five members of the first "Committee," or Board of Trustees, of the Hopkins Grammar School, now called Hopkins Academy. Mr. Judd, the accomplished historian of Hadley, speaks of him as an intelligent and influential man, and one qualified to do public business. The intimate friend of the minister, Mr. Russell, he was undoubtedly one of the few persons in Hadley to whom was entrusted the secret of concealment of the Regicides, Generals Whalley and Goffe, in Mr. Russell's house, for many years subsequent to 1664; and he may have witnessed the exploit of General Goffe, who is said to have emerged from his hiding place to save the panic stricken town from an attack of the Indians in September, 1675, an occurrence which the excitement of the occasion magnified into a supposed angelic visitation.*

The last year of the patriarch's life was full of trouble. It was then that King Philip's war burst upon the scattered settlements, and fell with special severity upon these remote towns of Hampshire. Two of his sons, Joseph and Azariah, fell that year, the former at Northfield with Capt. Beers, the latter in the "Swamp Fight" at Hatfield. The father, already stricken in years, did not long survive the double bereavement. He died at Hadley June 16, 1676.

The record of such a life, which filled so important a place in the settlement of this county, and which appears to have been enriched by useful and honorable deeds, deserves to be perpetuated. His numerous descendants, but a small fraction of whom are represented in this large gathering, will turn their thoughts hither to-day, and unite in doing honor to his memory. No pencil of artist has preserved to us the semblance of his features. Nothing remains from which we can even imagine how he looked. Not a single word that he ever spoke has come down to our day. No gravestone marks his resting place. We only know that he sleeps in the old burial ground in Hadley, but "no man knoweth his sepulchre unto this day." His monument, however, is not wanting. The memorials of our progenitor, and of the other good men with whom he was associated, in the settlement of Hadley, surround us on every side. We behold them in these fruitful farms, in these busy mills, and in these thriving communities. The prosperous churches, the noble charities, and the distinguished seats of learning, which have grown up within the limits of the original town, stand here as enduring witnesses of the courage and sacrifices of its founders. Yea, there is a memorial

*Sir Walter Scott repeats this tradition in "Peveril of the Peak," where he puts the story into the mouth of the Puritan hero, Major Bridgenorth.

even more imperishable than these. It is that reverential regard for the memory of the fathers, which, dwelling in the hearts of successive generations of their descendants, finds in the contemplation of ancestral virtues its most inspiring and ennobling lessons.

It is my privilege to welcome all to the profitable enjoyments of this occasion; and in doing this, let me express the hope that the reunion may stimulate a renewed interest in our family history, an honest pride in an honorable ancestry, a better acquaintance among our various branches, and above all, increasing devotion and loyalty to the principles of religious liberty and free government which were the inestimable gift of our English ancestry.

At the conclusion of the Address of Welcome, the audience joined in singing, to the tune of "Auld Lang Syne," the following lines by Mrs. Elizabeth Dickinson Currier, Worcester, Mass.:

 The day we celebrate, my friends,
  Is one of rarest kind,
 When Dickinsons with Dickinsons
  Sing auld lang syne.

   CHORUS.

  For auld lang syne, my frien's,
   For auld lang syne,
  We'll drink the health, long life and wealth,
   And days of auld lang syne.

When hearts to hearts together knit,
 And kindred hands clasp thine,
Then fill the cup with right good will,
 And sing of auld lang syne.—[CHORUS.

Let not this day be e'er forgot,
 But often brought to min',
And tak' a cup o' kindness e'er
 For auld lang syne.—[CHORUS.

The President.—As our common ancestor was a deacon, it was to be expected that the clergy would have a large representation among the Dickinsons. We therefore looked to this profession for the orator of the day, and I have the pleasure of introducing to you now Rev. Charles A. Dickinson, of Lowell, Massachusetts.

Rev. Charles A Dickinson then delivered the following Historical Address:

The Dickinson Family.

My Friends and Kinsmen:

Whether your name be Dickinson, Dickenson, Dickerson or Dickoson, I bring you greetings to-day from our common ancestors, among whose blessed shades I have been wandering for the past few months.

I have come to remind you of some things which you already know, and to tell you, perhaps, some things which you do not know.

You have, doubtless, all felt the power of that spell which is peculiar to the precincts of a picture gallery. You enter reverently, and with uncovered head look around upon the walls, where hang the faces of the world's heroes, saints and martyrs:—men and women great in deeds and great in character. You may be alone, and yet you do not seem to be alone : for you are surrounded by a cloud of witnesses. In whatever direction you cast your eyes, eyes look back into yours: stern eyes, tender eyes, prophetic eyes, sagacious eyes,—eyes which pierce you through and through, and make you feel like hiding yourself in some obscure nook of the gallery. And if you are gifted with the vision and the hearing which are born of a familiarity with history, those lips around you seem to move and speak, and to tell you stories of bygone days,—stories of struggle and toil and victory, which form no small part of the world's history. Through a single compartment of such a gallery I have been wandering in imagination for many weeks. I went in feeling very much as Topsy did when she declared that she had no ancestors; I came out feeling very much as the Chinaman must feel, the bulk of whose earthly possessions consists of the ponderous records of his pedigree and family history.

The faces which I have seen there form a mighty concourse. The stories which I have heard there would make a Dickinson cyclopædia.

I, of course, discovered among these faces, "My Lord" and "My Lady," for no family gallery would be complete without its modicum of nobility; and of course I encountered there the traditional shades of the "three brothers;" but when I attempted to detain them, like the ghost of Anchises, they escaped my hold, and in the place where they stood I saw no less than a dozen claimants of progenitorial honors. Out of the traditional and historical lore which I have found there, I have selected such fragments as may enable you to sketch for yourselves the outlines of our family tree.

We may congratulate ourselves that we have noble blood in our veins; not merely the blood of the Plantagenets, which has doubtless become rather thin by this time, but the blood of a sturdy, honest line of men and women who, though untitled and uncrowned, have possessed those qualities of mind and heart, without which the title and the crown would be but unsubstantial baubles.

HISTORICAL ADDRESS. 23

"Our boast is not that we deduce our birth
From loins enthroned, the rulers of the earth ;
But higher far our proud pretensions rise:
The sons of parents passed into the skies."

Our family, as it exists to-day, is the outgrowth of the climatic, social and moral conditions of four countries. Scandanavia, France, England and America have probably each had a moulding hand upon our physique and characters. Like all other families, we have our traditions ; and these tell us that among the bleak and windy hills of Northern Europe our pagan ancestors had their home in mediæval times. They belonged to that fierce, wild race which was known as Northmen, and were noted for their gigantic stature, enormous strength, and desperate bravery. They were made for war, and they loved war, and from their rocky fastnesses they made repeated invasions upon the neighboring nations. The most redoubtable of their invaders was Rolf or Rollo. He entered France early in the 10th century, wrested the land on either side of the Seine from the French King, Charles the Simple, was baptized, received the King's daughter in marriage and became his vassal for the territory, which then took the name of the Northman's land or Normandy. This Rollo, who was thus made the first Duke of Normandy, was the direct ancestor in the sixth generation of William the Conqueror, and, through a younger son, Walter, the reputed progenitor of the founder of the Dickinson family.

Walter, the son of Rollo, settled in Caen, a beautiful city of Normandy, at the junction of the Orne and the Odon. Here

"City and tower and castled wall
Were his estate."

And here for more than a century the family line was perpetuated. When William the Conqueror invaded

England, one of this noble line, Gautier de Caen, his kinsman, went with him and participated in that conquest which immortalized the name of the Norman.

Here tradition ceases for the most part, and history begins. The name of Walter of Caen appears among the Norman companions of the Conqueror, and also upon the battle roll of Hastings. According to an English record, in order to anglicize his name, he received a grant of land of the old Saxon manor of Kenson, which adjoins the little hamlet of that name, on the south branch of the Aire, near the City of Leeds, West Riding, Yorkshire. Here tradition tells us that Walter woed and wedded the daughter of the last Saxon Lord of Kenson. Sure it is he married some one, and had children, for his descendants remained Lords of this manor as late as the middle of the 17th century.

Here let us turn our attention for a moment to the derivation of our family name.

The various theories which have been suggested to me as to its origin are certainly ingenious and interesting, notwithstanding very few of them have been based on fact. We naturally feel that "our" way of spelling the name is the correct one, and as most of us have not been in the habit of ascending beyond our grandfather in the ancestral line, we are inclined to hold fast to the middle syllable which he gave us, and to regard the differing syllable which our kinsman's grandfather bequeathed to him as undoubtedly spurious. I dislike to feel that good Deacon Nathaniel was wrong for once in his life when he spelled his name with an "in;" but the facts seem to be against him, and all of his descendants. The "ens" have the right of it, I think, and can trace their orthography back in true Apostolic succession to the early fathers.

As to the derivation of the name, one friend assures us

that it was originally MacDickens, and that the Scotch prefix was in time superseded by its English equivalent, the suffix "son." Another holds the common idea that the family name was originally Dickens; while an English philologist affirms that we owe our nominal existence to Richard I., the faithless yet brilliant king who gave his name to a large number of English families. From Richard comes Dick or Diccon, says our writer, and from that comes Dickinson. Another theory is that as our race was of the City of Caen, in France, our remote ancestor may have been, for example, a John de Caen, and his sons may have been known as John de Caen's sons, which in time became Dickinson.

It has well been said of English surnames "that could we only grasp their meaning, could we take away the doubtful crust in which they are oftentimes embedded, then should we be speaking out of the very mouth of history itself." Our name is in a certain sense an epitome of our early history. Before the time of the Conqueror, it was not usual for surnames to descend from father to son, but each man had a sobriquet of his own. In the eleventh and twelfth centuries, however, a change took place, and a man's sobriquet became a part and parcel of his property, and was transmitted to his descendants. This appellation might be the designation of the property owned, of the craft pursued, or of the work or office of the individual.

As we have already seen, Walter of Caen took the name of his manor, and was known as Walter de Kenson, and in assuming this sobriquet, he wittingly or unwittingly recognized the three countries with which he and his ancestors had thus far had to do. The "son" happens to be a common ending of Danish and Swedish names, and tells of the rugged hills of Scandanavia, among which his forefathers worshipped the thunder god, pursued the chase and engaged in war. The prefix "de" tells of the less rugged country and the more civilized customs of fair Normandy, while the united syllables speak of the England of the Norman's adoption. Just when the family took the Anglicized form of the surname we cannot tell, but it was probably early in the 14th century. The two most ancient forms were (2) Dickensen, then Dicconson. Dickensen appears in the reign of Henry VII.; but it is not till a century later that we find the second syllable spelled with an "i," which is clearly a corruption of the original orthography.

All the ancient families of England had their Coats of Arms, and (3) that which adorned the Kenson manor house, and appeared upon the trappings and furniture of the earliest Dickinsons is doubtless before you to-day. "These arms," says Mr. Wharton Dickinson, who by the way, probably knows more about the English and Southern branches of our family than any other member of it, and to whom I am very largely indebted for my own knowledge concerning the origin of our family and its descent along the Anglo-Southern line,—"These arms," says he, "are certainly as old as the reign of Henry III., and they were certainly used by John de Caen of Kenson in the time of Edward I." They have an interesting story to tell concerning some of our ancestors. The green fields and the hinds' heads signify that the wearers were rangers in royal forests, most likely Epping in Yorkshire, which was established by William the Conqueror and his son, Rufus. The cross was not added till the time of the last crusade under Edward I., and signifies that some of the Dickinsons were engaged in that holy war. There are other Coats of Arms existing in the family, but they are of a later date. The design which we bear to-day was doubtless carried by Hugh Dicconsin, who lived about 1422, and who was probably the grandfather of John Dickenson of Leeds, the progenitor of all the American Dickinsons.

This John Dickenson, who died in 1525, was a younger son of the Lord of Kenson ; was a burgess and alderman of Leeds, and a successful wool merchant. His wife was Elizabeth, the daughter of Sir Robert Danby. How many children John and Elizabeth had I cannot say ; nor do I know whether the Southern and New England branches converge in them, or whether they find a common ancestor farther down the line. Among the children of John of Leeds, was a younger son William, who, in 1525, left his native city and moved to Bradley, in Staffordshire, where he married Rachael Kinge, and became the founder of the well-known family of Bradley Dickinsons, many of whom have won their laurels, and made their mark upon the times in which they lived. To William and Rachael was born Richard, who married Eliza Bagnall. It is quite probable that these two descendants of John of Leeds, William and Richard, had other children than those mentioned, whose offspring are scattered to-day throughout England and America ; but I am unable to trace them. The only unbroken line which has come to my knowlege is that of the Southern branch of our family, the members of which are able to trace their lineage directly back to Symon, (4) the son of Richard and Eliza.

This Symon, the great-grandson of John of Leeds, lived at Bradley during the brilliant reign of Elizabeth, and married Catherine, the daughter of Geoffrey Sutton and the grand-daughter of (5) Lord Dudley, thus allying himself with the royal family of the (6) Plantagenets. Their children were Charles and William and Edward, two, and possibly all of whom were the progenitors of a very large division of our family in this country.

Having thus considered the root and the main trunk of our genealogical tree as it flourished in England, we will turn our thoughts to the various branches which appeared on this side of the water.

It is impossible to say how many of our name have emigrated to this country ; but a glance at a published list of those who embarked from the old country to the new during the 17th century will convince us that descendants of the well-known emigrants have by no means a monopoly of the Dickinson blood. Virginia seems to have been a favorite point of destination for many of the name. I find that in 1620 Jeremiah Dickinson embarked from England to that State in the good ship *Margett* and *John*, at the age of 26. He was followed in 1623 by Elizabeth Dickinson, whose age was 38. George Dickinson, a young man of 19, and William, aged 21, came from London to Virginia in 1635, and then there were Florence, and Joe, and John, who took passage during the same year.

These are but a few of our name which occurs again and again in these voluminous records of England's direct contributions to America's population. They are the forgotten members of our family, who lived and loved and died in this the country of their adoption. Silently and inconspicuously they did their part towards introducing into the warp and woof of our national life the substantial threads of the family character. We may not be able to discover or trace those threads to-day; nevertheless they are there. Among the other emigrants, concerning whom I have little knowledge save the fact and the date of their emigration may be mentioned, Jonathan of Jamaica, in the West Indies, who came to Philadelphia about 1700, and was Mayor of that city and Judge of the Supreme Court of Pennsylvania ; and Joseph, the ancestor of the celebrated Anna Dickinson, who came over in 1747. The few emigrants who were fortunate enough to perpetuate their memory among their descendants, and who became the founders of some of the well-known branches of our family in this country must claim our attention at this time. And we will begin with that branch which can trace its line in direct male descent from the founder of the family in England.

One of the sons of Symon Dickinson and Catherine Dudley was Charles, a merchant, who lived in London and died in 1653. Rachael Carter was his wife, and his sons were Walter, Henry and John, all of whom emigrated to Virginia in 1654, bearing within them germs of talent which, in their descendants, were destined to develop and blossom with remarkable luxuriance under the conditions of the new world. Of these three sons, Walter, who married for his first wife Jane Yarrett, moved to Talbot County, in Maryland, and there became the founder of the Talbot Dickinsons, so many of whom have gained distinction in political, military, literary and social pursuits. Mr. Wharton Dickinson, the genealogist of our Southern branch, who I am happy to say is with us to-day, belongs to this line. And here also we find the legitimate head of the entire Dickinson race, in the person of Mr. Samuel T. Dickinson, who lives upon the ancestral estate in Talbot County, Md., and who is able to trace his ancestry along the elder line of thirteen generations to the man who first bore the Dickinson name. He doubtless appreciates the honors of his distinguished position, and bears them with becoming dignity.

Turning now to Henry, the second son of Charles of London, we find that he married a Miss Jennings and settled in what is now known as Old Virginia, where he became the patriarch of the Virginia Dickensons, and also the progenitor of some of the families which are found in Alabama and other Southern States. The Virginia family has been noted for its valor ; has suffered much at the hands of the red man ; has had representatives in all of the wars of the Republic, and through all the corrupting influences of the times has clung with loyal devotion to the ancestral "e" in its nominal orthography.

A third son of Charles of London was John, who moved from Virginia, and through his son William became the ancestor of a large branch of the Pennsylvania Dickinsons, many of whose names are synonyms for some of the most sterling virtues which have distinguished our race.

To return again to Symon of Bradley and his gentle lady Catherine; we find that they had a son William, who was rector of Appleton, in Berkshire, and who by his wife, Mary Culpepper, had at least six children, among whom were Francis, the ancestor of the Dickinsons of King Weston, Somersetshire, and of Trinity House, London; Edmund, the celebrated physician; and William of Abingdon, who I am inclined to think was the ancestor of the so-called Scotch Dickinsons, and also the Rowley Dickinsons in this country. It is reported that Thomas, a son of his, lived and died on the banks of the bonny Ayr in Scotland, and left Moses and Thomas and Josiah, who came to America in 1690, and settled near Deerfield, in this State. Moses was the ancestor of General Leonard A. Dickinson of Hartford, Conn. and the Rev. Legh Richmond Dickinson, now of Pennsylvania; and Thomas had for an illustrious descendant the Hon. Daniel S. Dickinson, (7) of New York. The Scotch cousins seemed, like their kinsmen, to possess sound minds in sound bodies; and not a few of them kept death waiting at the door a long while after his time-piece had struck the allotted three score and ten. One member of the family, Reuben, a grandson of Moses, outlived by four years the century which was born with him, and his 100th birthday was celebrated by a special service in Trinity Church, Milton, Conn., the choir singing "Old Hundred" as he walked up the aisle. He was asked on that day to mow a swath of hay in his meadow, but he declined, saying, "No, it will look like taking to myself the glory of my health and strength, when it all belongs to God."

On the 10th of May, 1637, there embarked on the ship *Mary Ann* from Yarmouth, England, one (8) Philemon Dickerson in company with Benj. Cooper, his employer. He was a tanner by trade, and he settled in Salem, where as I suppose he had a grant of land in 1637. He was made a freeman in 1641, and in the same year married Mary, the daughter of Thomas Payne of Salem, and had baptized in that town Mary, on the 20th of March, 1642, and Thomas, on the 10th of March, 1644.

Owing to the conflicting statements which I have received I am unable to say just when he left Salem, but it seems that he finally settled in Southold, Long Island, and that his will was presented in New York, where his widow was made administratrix, October 28th, 1672. His peculiar spelling of our name is found in the returns from the Custom House at Yarmouth, the port from which he sailed, and is still preserved among his descendants, who are very numerous in New York, Pennsylvania and New Jersey, and have had the distinguished honor of giving to the latter State two Governors, in the persons of the two brothers, Mahlon (9) and Philemon (10).

Passing on to still another fragment of our family history, we learn that somewhat more than a century and a half ago there lived in England a Charles or James Dickinson, who was a minister of the Church of England in Northumberland County, and whose family were in possession of a great portion of White Haven. His son, Stewart Dickinson, entered Ireland with Oliver Cromwell, gained an estate in Westmeath called Stone Hall, and settling there, married Lady Talbot, by whom he had four sons, one of whom, James, married Hannah Smith in Dublin. Two of their sons, John and James, emigrated to this country, the former making his home in Pittsburg, where he set up the first power weaving loom in Pennsylvania. Some of the descendants of the latter are now living in Hoboken.

But I know that you are anticipating the mention of another name which is sacred to every New England Dickinson who is acquainted with his family history,—a name which now as in the days when the man "without guile" sat under the fig tree, is a synonym for integrity. Many a time these ancient hills and vales have resounded to the name of Nathaniel Dickinson, but only, as we believe, to send back the echo that he was one of Nature's noble men.

His early home was England, but who blessed his home for him we cannot tell. In his antecedents he is to us like Melchizedek, "without father, without mother, and without descent;" but in his subsequent history he is a veritable Abraham, for "his seed is as the sand of the desert, which cannot be numbered for multitude." That he is a scion of the common tree we have no doubt. The recurrence of the names Charles, Daniel, John, Elijah, Nathaniel, Samuel and William in the English, New England and Southern branches, clearly indicate a common origin. It is said that Jonathan Dickinson, (11) a President of Princeton College, located the English home of Nathaniel on the Isle of Ely in Cambridge; but I am more inclined to trust the evidence which locates it in Hadleigh, Suffolkshire. There, I believe, under the influence of a Christian home, he laid the foundations of that sturdy character which was to make him a power in his day and generation, and which, transmitted from father to son, was to form no small part of the vertebral force of New England. A young man in the most delightful flower of his age, with nerves unshattered by dissipation, and a character strong in the Lord, he in company with many others embarked at Gravesend in the year 1629 or 1630, and turned his face to the land of promise. Whether he bore his hopes alone to the new world, or whether he shared them on his voyage with Anna Gull we cannot say. We only are sure that this youthful widow became his wife about this time, either in England or America, and that she was in all respects worthy of the name which he gave her.

Upon his arrival at Boston it is reported that he settled in Watertown, where were born to him John and Joseph and Thomas, the worthy first fruits of the New England stock.

The East winds, however, probably did not agree with him; for we find him moving Westward, and in 1637, erecting his family altar in Wethersfield, Conn., a town which, not slow to discover and appreciate his worth, honored him with her highest confidence, making him her Recording Clerk in 1645, and her Representative during the ten following years, at the end of which time a stiff Theological breeze springing up in the church at Hartford, struck the church at Wethersfield, and drove the Dickinson family ship to the Northward. The Dickinsons have always been noted for having a mind of their own, and never has their opinionativeness been more manifest than when it has concerned religious matters. Whether churchmen or anti-churchmen, our fathers have always been independent leading spirits. An old historian of Leeds, who was evidently not a non-conformist, in speaking of an uprising of that party in the West Riding of Yorkshire, says "A misguided and enthusiastic rabble met in Farley Wood for the purpose of overturning the existing government, and declaring for a Christian magistracy and a gospel ministry, and among their leaders was William Dickinson. * * * John Dickinson was also a carrier on of the design, and a certain Luke Lunt testified that he desired to be a Captain."

It was evidently a non-conformist spirit which inspired Nathaniel and others of the Wethersfield church, who, as strict Congregationalists, could not conscientiously submit to certain innovations which the majority attempted to impose upon them. Wearied at length with the controversy, and at the same time attracted by the beautiful and fertile fields which lay farther up the Connecticut, he eagerly joined in a movement which had for its object the purchase and settlement of a tract of land in the valley of Norwottuck. This was accomplished in 1659, and he and fifty-nine other "engagers," taking possession of the region, gave to it the name of Hadley, after the name which was dear to many of them in Old England.

Beautiful for situation was Norwottuck, with its broad plains still unreclaimed, flanked on the one side by its mountain fortress, and laved on the other by the waters of the Connecticut. There was life in its soil. There was health in its atmosphere; but then, there were Indians and wolves in its woods, and hardships under every square foot of its alluvial plains. He who would possess the land must have a brave heart and a strong right arm.

It is a patriarchal family which folds up its tents in Wethersfield to pitch them again in Norwottuck :—a family which foes, physical and spiritual, have each, doubtless, good reason to fear. The patriarch himself is in the prime and vigor of life, and following him are his worthy wife, nine strapping sons and two fair daughters ; the eldest of the sons, John, bringing with him as his wife the daughter of Nathaniel Foote, of Wethersfield, who is the proud mother of six small children. Among these twenty Dickinsons are seven men over eighteen years of age, who can swing an axe or handle a musket with equal facility.

The town plot of Hadley was laid out in four quarters, two on each side of the street, divided by a highway ; and it was agreed that each home-lot should contain eight acres. In the allotment of these homesteads Nathaniel received the one in the extreme southeast of the town ; Thomas, who, I suppose, being still unmarried, lived with his father, received the lot adjoining this ; and John took a lot farther up the street, just below the lot of Richard

Montague, whose descendants held their family meeting in Hadley last year, and to the earnest efforts of one of whom, in connection with those of our indefatigable secretary, the success of this meeting is largely due. This proximity of the Dickinsons and the Montagues, by the way, has been perpetuated by Irene and Luke, who in their children and children's children have forever united the blood of Nathaniel and Richard. Here over the ground which, with its carpet of green, and its double vista of patriarchal elms, is to-day one of the most picturesque streets in the world. Nathaniel and the children who have come after him have passed and re-passed till every foot of the soil has become sacred to him who bears the family name. Here were formed those attachments, here were imbibed those principles which determined the very existence and character of many who are assembled here to-day. Nathaniel was evidently a leading man in Hadley, as he had been in Wethersfield. He held many public offices, and devoted himself to the public weal. The Hadley Church made him one of its first deacons, and found in him a staunch supporter. A meeting-house had to be erected, of course, and Goodman Dickinson was one of the seven who were chosen by the town to build it. When it was completed the town voted: "That there should be some sticks set up in the meeting-house in several places, with some fit persons placed by them, and to use them as occasion shall require to keep the youths from disorder." Whether Deacon Dickinson was an advocate of this Solomonic method of correcting the manners of the young Hadlians we cannot tell, but we do know that his interest in the young went farther than that of a tithing man, and led him to devote himself with unflagging zeal to their intellectual welfare. He was one of the five "able and pious men" chosen by the town to take charge of the Hopkins bequest, which was given "for the breeding up of hopeful youths in a way of learning, both at the grammar school and college." He had a hand in building the school-house, and served for several years on the school committee. In the school which was thus established, and in the interest which Nathaniel and his cotemporaries took in the subject of education, we have the beginning of those influences which have resulted in making this surrounding region, and especially this classic height upon which we are now gathered, one of the great educational centres of our land. The church, the school, and the town-meeting, the three foundation stones of our American Independence, each found an early and sure establishment in Hadley, and, so far as we know, an earnest guardian in every Dickinson.

Nathaniel did not reside continually in Hadley, but spent a part of his declining years in Northampton and Hatfield; but upon the death, perhaps, of his good wife, Anna, he returned again to his kinspeople, and there, on the 16th of June, 1676, he died, being full of years and faith. Somewhere in the Norwottuck valley, over against yonder mountain, he lies buried, (12) "but no man knoweth of his sepulchre unto this day."

The time would fail me to tell of John, and Joseph, and Thomas, and Samuel, and Obadiah, and Nathaniel, and Nehemiah, and Hezekiah, and Azariah, and Anna, and Frances, the eleven children of the Patriarch, all of whom have called some place within the circle of these hills their home, and ten of whom have probably some living representatives in this county to-day.

These ten members of the present generation took to themselves companions and became the parents of about seventy children, who have each done his part toward perpetuating the name and fame of the New England branch.

John, the oldest son, as we have already seen, wedded Frances Foote at the early age of sixteen or seventeen, and became the father of six children before he was twenty-seven.

Joseph, the second son, married Phœbe Bracy at Hartford, by whom he had six children.

The death of Joseph suggests a strange fatality which seemed to follow our family during its early New England history. While attempting, in company with Capt. Beers and thirty-six others, to rescue a garrison at Northfield, he was set upon by a great number of Indians from a swamp and killed. He seems to be the first of a large company of Hadley Dickinsons who suffered and died under the ruthless hand of the savage. The names Benoni and Captivity, which we find in our family records, are the sad reminders of these sufferings, and upon a hillside in Northfield is a monument, which, though erected in memory of a single victim of the red man's cruelty, may well be regarded as commemorating a long succession of calamities of which his death was a type. On the monument, which was erected by Mr. Elijah Dickinson, of Fitchburg, and a few others, we read:

Nathaniel Dickinson
was killed
and scalped
by the Indians,
at this place,
April 15, 1747,
aged 48.

The history which lies back of that inscription is full of tears and heart-pangs. Martha, the loving wife, surrounded by her children, was waiting in the old fort-home for the return of her husband; but there were no tidings till the faithful old family horse, led by kind and sorrowing neighbors, ascended the hill and halted with his lifeless burden before the door. On the following December the stricken widow gave birth to a son, and she called his name Benoni—the son of my sorrow. He grew to manhood, but he could never handle a musket or listen to a tale of Indian warfare.

But we have wandered. The third son of Nathaniel was Thomas, who took for his wife Elizabeth Crow, of Hadley. His home-lot was next to his father's; but in 1679 he disposed of it and moved to Wethersfield, where he died in 1716, leaving eight children. I find that Thomas was one of the noted wolf hunters of his town, which in those days was no small honor, for wolves were very common and destructive, and they tried the patience of the settlers to the utmost. A writer in 1634 considered them "the greatest inconveniency in the county," and liberal rewards were offered for their capture.

One of these ferocious animals became quite a Nemesis upon one occasion, and thus played an important part in the moral discipline of a young scion of our family. It came about in this way: Perez, a son of Nathan, of Amherst, was a good boy, but like all other boys of that day, he was a little restive under some of the religious restrictions of his Puritan home. On one Thanksgiving Day, having been kept in decorous quiet within doors, according to the usual custom, until his young limbs fairly ached for a wrestle or a game at fisticuffs, he took occasion at evening prayers to steal away from the family, and started off to see neighbor Hastings's boys, who lived a mile away. Just as he was entering a dark piece of woods he saw in the distance an object which thrilled him with terror. It was an ugly-looking wolf in quest of a Thanksgiving supper. Poor Perez! His guilty heart stood still. He thought of his naughtiness, and of the bears in the Bible, who made a supper of the other naughty boys. He ran, and the wolf ran; and the faster he ran, the more certain was he that he was pursued by the justice of Heaven. Fortunately, the home door cut off the threatened retribution, however, and its latch fell just as the feet of the hungry avenger came scratching against it. The lesson was never forgotten, and one wolf at least did good service in a good cause.

But returning again to the family of Nathaniel, we notice that (13) Samuel, his fourth son, married Martha Bridgman, of Springfield, and settled in Hartford, where he died at the age of 73. He had nine children, three of whom, Samuel, Nathaniel and Ebenezer, took an active part in that fearful battle of Deerfield Meadows, in 1704.

Obadiah, another son, married for his first wife Sarah Beardsley, and for his second wife Mehitable Johnson. He also settled in Hatfield, but was soon unsettled by the Indians, who burned his house, wounded his wife, and carried himself and child to Canada. He was ransomed the following year, and finally removed to Wethersfield, where he died in 1698. Four sons and two daughters kept his memory green.

Another son of the pioneer was named after his father. He was married three times, and was the father of six children, several of whom had a sorry time of it with the pestiferous red-skins. One son, Nathaniel, had his horse shot from under him, and had one boy killed while hoeing corn, and another carried away captive, while the wife of another son, John, was tomahawked and left for dead amid the ruins of her home.

If you go into the southeast corner of the old Hadley burying-ground, you will see there a brown head-stone. It is over-grown with lichens, but a careful scrutiny will reveal the name of Lieutenant Nehemiah Dickinson, another son of Nathaniel, and a twin brother of Nathaniel, Jr., who, as it appears, in his younger days was somewhat given to the vanities of life.

There was a law at that time in Massachusetts ordering "that persons whose estates did not exceed 200 pounds should not wear gold or silver lace, gold or silver buttons, bone lace above two shillings a yard, or silk hoods or scarfs, upon penalty of ten shillings for every offence."

At the March court in 1676 the jury presented thirty-eight maids and wives, and thirty young men. "Some for wearing silk in a flaunting manner, and others for long hair and other extravagances," and our Lieutenant Nehemiah was among them. He had probably shocked the sensibilities of the good people of Hadley, and incurred the stern displeasure of the law by indulging in the traditional weakness of his sex—a red necktie.

Poor Lieutenant Nehemiah! It is unfortunate that that one bit of extravagance should be the only thing by which he is destined to be known to posterity. Aside from this and his epitaph, his record is a blank. A single foible outlives the virtues of a lifetime. His tendencies to these frivolities, however, did not appear to abate his natural vigor or shorten his life, for he reared fourteen children and died at the age of 80; and his blood to-day, mingled with that of other Puritan stock, flows in the veins of some of the most worthy citizens of our land.

Hezekiah, his brother, was a merchant in Hatfield, Hadley, and finally at Springfield, where he died in 1707. Abigail Blackman shared his fortunes and bore him six children, among whom was Jonathan, the first president of Princeton College, and Moses, who became an able clergyman in Norwalk, Connecticut.

The ninth and last son of Deacon Nathaniel was Azariah, who settled in the northern part of Hatfield, and was killed by the Indians in 1675.

Of the two daughters of Nathaniel, Anna married for her first husband John Clary, and being left a widow she married Enos Kingsley. Frances appears to have died unmarried. She was the last of the second generation, and with her we must complete our sketch of the New England branch, although it would be interesting to follow the history into later times.

A little daughter of our worthy secretary, upon being asked, not long ago, whether she was a Republican or a Democrat, replied with a good deal of spirit: "I am neither, sir; I am a Dickinson." We feel to-day very much as she felt. We are neither New Englanders, New Yorkers, nor Pennsylvanians; neither Episcopalians, Congregationalists, Baptists, nor Presbyterians; but we are all Dickinsons, and as such we are interested in every member of the family who has brought honor to our name, whether he has lived North, South, East or West. To tell you what our family has done for the world, through its representative men, would be impossible. We can only turn our thoughts to a few of the great names which illumine our page of history.

Could John of Leeds have caught a glimpse of his distinguished progeny through some Banquo's wizard glass, his family pride would have suffered an inflation which might have been disastrous. There have probably been some Don Quixotes, some Sancho Panzas, some Shylocks, perhaps, and some Iagos among his descendants, but if there have been their memory has been lost. The only disreputable character which I have been able to find is one Dickey Dickinson, of England, who kept an inn and gained quite a notoriety as a clown and a punster.

To quote again from Mr. Wharton Dickinson, he says: "I think the family to which we belong may feel a just pride in the record of our ancestors. I have yet to find anything mean or ignoble connected with any of the various branches, from the earliest to the present time. They have been a race of earnest, honest, God-fearing men; oftentimes men of ability, and sometimes great scholars."

In religious matters the Dickinsons have been good church men, good Puritans, and good Quakers. If there is such a thing as religiosity, many, especially in the New England branch, have possessed a good deal of it. In all church matters they have been first and foremost, so that in some localities, as I am told, the phrase "Deacon Dickinson" is as familiar as the sound of the church bell. Among the great company of faithful clergymen who have honored our name, and who are now in the church triumphant, we find the name of Timothy, (14) whose quiet, unpretentious life in the little town of Holliston is full of the beauty of holiness. To my own mind he was an ideal minister, being truly great in all of those qualities which most become the man of God. He also seemed to possess to a large degree the sterling characteristics of the family—determination, perseverance, courage, integrity, and to represent them toned and glorified within the atmosphere of a love which thought no evil. He was a descendant of Nathaniel. He served his church for 24 years, and died in 1813 at the age of 52.

As we have already seen, the cause of education has found among our kith and kin some of its staunchest supporters. Dickinson College, in Pennsylvania, which was founded in 1783, was named for John Dickinson, (15) "in memory of the great and important services rendered to his country, and in recognition of his very liberal donation to the institution." One of the founders of Amherst College was the Hon. Samuel Fowler Dickinson, (16) an eminent lawyer, whose name was associated with every public interest and benevolent enterprise in his town and county. And to the interest of the Rev. Austin Dickinson, (17) and the disinterested efforts of his distinguished brother, Baxter Dickinson, D. D., (18) that same college was indebted for no small part of its financial strength during its early history. Deerfield Academy owes its existence to a Dickinson, and Mobile Academy was some time conducted most successfully by Deborah, a daughter of the Rev. Symeon Dickinson, of Haddam.

Some of the most worthy and influential members of our family have belonged to the Society of Friends, and have therefore been averse to the smell of gunpowder and

the clash of arms; but there are other members who have
proved themselves to be the veritable sons of Mars.
They have pursued the red man, conquered the red coat,
and fought with equal intrepidity under the blue and
under the gray, and they have won by their valor every
military title from Lieutenant to General. Your already
wearied patience would be quite exhausted should I attempt
to call the roll of our heroes this morning, and so I
will only speak of two or three of them. One of the most
noted of our soldiers was General Philemon, (19) a descendant
of Walter, of the Southern line. Born on his father's
plantation, Croise-dore, Talbot County, Maryland, April
15, 1739, he graduated from Philadelphia College in 1757
and began the study of law. In 1775 he was made Colonel
of one of the ten battallions of infantry which the
Provincial Congress of New Jersey raised for the defense
of the State. Soon exchanging the title of Colonel for
that of Brigadier-General, Philemon became actively engaged
in the war of the Revolution, and by his coolness,
skill and bravery, soon placed himself among the most
successful officers of the army. General Washington
wrote concerning an action of his on the banks of the Millstone
River: "General Dickinson's behavior reflects the
highest credit on him, for, though his troops were all
new, he led them through the river middle deep, under a
severe fire, and gave the enemy so severe a charge that,
although they were supported by three field pieces, they
gave way, left their convoy and fled."

General Philemon supplemented his military career
with a political career no less brilliant, and died in his
seventieth year.

Of the many Revolutionary heroes of the New England
branch, Captain Reuben, of Amherst, was one of the most
distinguished. Upon receiving the news of the battle of
Lexington, he rallied his company of Minute Men, twenty-eight
of whom were from Amherst, and seven of whom

were Dickinsons, and hastened at once to the scene of the conflict, where he did valiant service in routing the British. He and his company were in the thickest of the fray at Bunker Hill, and they also participated in all the hardships and the glory of the campaign which ended the war.

A kinsman, writing from Russel county, Virginia, says: "The only thing urged against one of us when aspiring to any position of trust or profit, is that the Dickinsons have had everything." We have but to glance at the political records of our family to be impressed with the fact that the Dickinsons have everywhere had their full share of civic honors, and I have yet to hear of one who has betrayed his trust or disgraced his office. No history of our country would be complete without something more than a passing allusion to Governor John Dickinson, the patriot and statesman of Revolutionary fame. Perhaps it would not be invidious to say that, all things considered, he was the greatest of the American Dickinsons, and one of the most distinguished men of his age. He was a brother of General Philemon, and a great-grandson of Walter. He was born at Croise-dore, in Talbot county, Maryland, in 1732, and in the course of his remarkable life he was Speaker of the Delaware Assembly, member of the Pennsylvania Assembly, of the Stamp Act Congress, of the Provincial Congress, of the Convention of Pennsylvania, of the Continental Congress, and of the Council of Safety. He was Justice of the Peace, Deputy Attorney General of Pennsylvania, Vice-President of the Delaware Council, Chief Justice of the High Court of Appeals, President of Delaware, President of Pennsylvania, Chairman of the Annapolis Convention, Member of the Federal Constitutional Convention, Trustee of the University of Pennsylvania, founder of Dickinson College, and Colonel and Brigadier-General of Militia. It was he who said: "I would like to make a great bustle in the world if it could be done by virtuous actions." And he did it.

Not far below the name of John should be written the name of Daniel Stevens Dickinson, of New York. The laurel which adorned the brow of the one would well become the other. Daniel belonged to the so-called Scotch family. He was born at Goshen, Connecticut, in 1807, and in his early life tilled the soil. But one day, not long after his marriage, he came into the house, put down with a decisive gesture the axe which he had been using, and declared that he would fit himself for the law. This he did, and in due time took the position for which his great talents qualified him. One office after another was conferred upon him, and he speedily became the acknowledged leader of his party. He was State Senator, Lieutenant Governor, United States Senator, and was elected by one hundred thousand majority to the Attorney-Generalship of New York in 1861, and in 1864 was prominently presented by the press throughout the country for the office of Vice-President of the United States. He received a flattering vote, but unfortunately Andrew Johnson was nominated. As a debater, Mr. Dickinson occupied the front rank in the forum. As an orator, he was peerless. As a writer, he was clear and forcible. As a poet, he was charming. As a man, to use the words which (20) Daniel Webster himself applied to him, he was "noble, able, manly and patriotic."

The name of (21) Dr. Edmund Dickinson, of England, suggests a profession which has been honored by not a few of that celebrated physician's kinsmen. He was a surgeon of extraordinary skill, and was entrusted with the health of King Charles himself. In the early history of our own country, when medical colleges were few, there was a species of semi-doctor which was quite common in New England. A smattering of physic, a knowledge of the names of herbs, a fair share of self-assurance, and a few happy recoveries in spite of concoctions, plasters and lancet, would give a man quite a reputation as a physician. Report says that one Ebenezer, of our line, though not educated as a doctor, made a specialty of canker, rash and rattles, using roots and herbs mixed with rattlesnake's gall and oil as remedies. His school has doubtless become extinct, and his descendants, if any of them are engaged in the healing art, are doubtless practicing a better way. Sure it is, that many of our line have been, and are to-day, worthy successors of Dr. Edmund; and one of them we shall have the pleasure of hearing from upon this occasion, in the person of the venerable Dr. Corson, who, although he calls himself "a pure, unadulterated, country doctor, who has never had a sign," has nevertheless received the highest honors of his profession.

You are asking by this time if the list is not exhausted. By no means. There are more to come. It was the celebrated artist, Gilbert Stuart, who said that he got his living by making faces. Well, we have a Dickinson who got at least a part of his living by making Gilbert Stuart's face, and he was the only artist who was ever allowed to have that honor. His name was Anson, (22) and he descended from Moses, the eldest of the three brothers who came from Scotland in 1670. He lived at Albany and in New York, and attained great celebrity as a miniature painter. Washington Irving, in a (23) letter to a friend, says of him: "He is an artist of highly promising talents, and of most amiable demeanor and engaging manners. He is not a mere mechanic in his art, but paints from his imagination. He has lately executed a figure of Hope, which does great credit to his invention and execution, and bespeaks a most delicate and classic taste. How I would glory in being a man of opulence, to take such young artists by the hand and cherish their budding genius."

Daniel, the brother of Anson, though less noted, won an enviable reputation in the same art.

The number of our distinguished dead is so great that I have deemed it my duty to speak of them, rather than of the living. It would hardly seem that such men as John, and Philemon, and Mahlon, and Nathaniel, would need the service of so poor a pen as mine to recall them to the memory of their kindred. And yet how many of us had heard of them six months ago? In the rush and whirl of our busy lives, the past is easily forgotten, and the wires are cut which might bring to us the electric stimulus of those characters which are below the horizon of to-day. As we have seen, it is a noble company which has passed over that vanishing line. And the half has not been told. The great, unnamed multitude lies over there in the dim shadows: Farmers, mechanics, tradesmen, who served well their day and generation; fathers and mothers, who were content to walk in sequestered ways, and to work for the world through the children whom they reared. Yes, it is a noble company. Men and women of high degree and low estate; men and women true and faithful, who have done their work well, adorned their age and left to their posterity that good name which is rather to be chosen than great riches. Theirs were the bright colors, and for a scutcheon they had the crusader's cross. Theirs were the housings upon which were written: "Love to God and man." Theirs the banner on which was inscribed: "To be rather than to appear."

Yes, there were giants in those days. But, my kinsmen, let us not commit the error of thinking that the race is extinct.

> "The fathers sleep; but men remain
> As wise, as true, as brave as they;
> Why count the loss, and not the gain?
> The best is that we have to-day."

It is not for me to eulogize the living, but pardon me for asking: What production of our past has been more tender than that poem, entitled, "The Children," (24) which has a world-wide celebrity, and which was composed by our Binghamton editor? What hymns have brought more comfort to the Christian heart than those which have been sung by our (25) Pennsylvania rector? What legal ability of the past has exceeded that which to-day under our name graces the bar in Boston and New York, and the bench in Pennsylvania, Virginia and Maryland? What editorial pen has been more vigorous than those which to-day control two of the most widely circulated religious papers of our country?—the *Religious Herald*, of Richmond, and the New York *Evangelist*. What family, descended from John of Leeds, has done more for the age in which they have lived than those four sons of their noble mother, one of whom is the editor just referred to in New York; another of whom planned and laid the first Atlantic cable; a third of whom is an eminent lawyer, and the fourth of whom is on the Supreme bench at Washington? (26)

But why do I specify? There has been a deluge since the days of Nathaniel and Walter, and the Rappahannock and Connecticut have overflown their banks, bearing the Dickinson family arks into about every State in the Union, and leaving so many of our cotemporary kinsmen stranded not only upon the Ararat of social and civil distinction, but also along the respectable table-lands of life, that to designate a few would be an injustice to the multitude.

But what of our future? Our future! Where is it? It is in the Dickinson Home, which now, as in the days of our fathers, is the sacred conservatory of the family character. In our children who romp at the firesides, and gather around the family board,

"As if fair Ariadne's crown
Out of the sky had fallen down."

These blithe-hearted little ones are great now only in confiding trust and innocence; but theirs, after all, is a greatness before which we bring our deepest homage, while we pray that it may never be superseded by that which is of the earth earthy. They are not as numerous in the individual household now as they were in the days of Lieutenant Nehemiah, but that I suppose is because there are more households to share them. They are a goodly company, however, and we need fear no disastrous uprising of the beam if we drop them into the scale of the future over against our ancestors.

Ah, John and Elizabeth, ye who in the distant past made for the Dickinson household a place among the myriad homes of earth, come back to us upon this auspicious occasion, look into our cradles and our nurseries, look into the faces of our young men and maidens, and tell us if the former days were any more full of promise than the present. They seem to come

> That ancient bridegroom and his bride,
> "Smiling, contented and serene,
> Upon the blithe, bewildering scene,
> And see, well-pleased, on every side,
> Their forms and features multiplied,
> As the reflection of a light
> Between two burnished mirrors gleams,
> Or lamps upon a bridge at night
> Stretch on and on before the sight,
> Till the long vista endless seems."

The President—I am sure that I but express the unanimous feeling of this audience in saying that whatever else our committee may have done, they certainly deserve our thanks for the selection they made for the delivery of the historical address. [Applause.]

The audience then united in singing the following song, by Alice E. Dickinson, Hadley, Mass.:

Tune—Heber.

A dazzling splendor meets the eye;
  On hillside and on plain,
On every side is bending low
  The ripe and golden grain.

In sunlit glade and leafy grove,
  The glad birds seem to sing
That Harvest doth again fulfill
  The prophecies of Spring.

In weakness striving to attain
  That love that knows no fear,
In faith and hope our fathers strewed
  The seeds of freedom here.

Bedewed with tears, enriched by prayer,
  The ever-fruitful sod
Yields us the meed of others' toil,—
  Free right to worship God.

Beside all waters where they sowed
  Behold the ripe increase,
The sheaves of liberty and love,
  The harvest-time of peace!

Rev. Chas. A. Dickinson then read the following poem, by Mrs. Elizabeth Dickinson Currier:

PROLOGUE OR APOLOGY.

Mr. Secretary—
  You asked me for "a hymn or two,"
  To sing, or read, this day in view,
  When Dickinsons with Dickinsons

Should try their lances, swords and guns.
At once I said—the gift divine,
Of Poesy—was never mine,
For oft my Muse was coaxed and bid,
Hoping to find in corner hid,
Some spark of genius, or of fire,
To gratify my heart's desire,
In writing words of holy cheer
For suffering souls both far and near.
But—like a woman off her knees,
"Uncertain—coy—and hard to please,"
She, laughing ever, mocked my pain,
And bade me never try again.
But then you said—that's no excuse,
"Try, try again," nor e'er refuse
To look an effort in the face,
For I am sure you'll "win the case."
So, with this flatt'ring compliment
I set to work, but ne'er was sent
One heavenly breath from Orpheus' lyre,
Worthy the day—worthy my sire,
For you have often heard it said,
And from the Poet, too, have read:
A "woman's *will*—you may depend on't,"
And, too, her "*won't*"—and there's the end on't.
My Muse has some of woman's "won't,"
And stubborn says—and "there's the end on't."

    I much deplore my want of art,
    To write a Poem—or impart
    Some graceful feature to this Day,
    But let that be such as it may—
    When *gifts are wanting*—'tis no use
    To waste our time in harsh abuse,
    Or even dare to question "why"
    Our Pegasus though winged, "won't" fly.

And though my thanks are weak and lame,
For asking something for my *Name*,
I fain must dry my streaming eyes,
And see another win the prize.

But—rather than the meed decline,
I venture forth this song of mine,
For vict'ries gained, are, to my eyes,
A ladder leading to the skies.

POEM.

A king to neighbor king once sent—
  "Come, let us see each other's face."
Like message, with a like intent,
  Has caused the gathering in this place.

No "Barmecide," with shadowy feast,
  Summons by bugle-call to-day;
From south, from north, from west, from east,
  These Dickinsons in full array.

No "Barmecide" shall here preside,
  To mock us with elusive fare;
But all "the good the gods provide,"
  Shall whet our appetite to share.

And what "the good," and who the guests?
  Are questions you will surely ask;
We straight will answer these requests,
  Nor deem it any onerous task.

And first the "good." Can better be
  Than "blood that tells"—inherited?
A deep and strong mentality
  To every "branch" accredited?

A brain well trained to think and act,
  A tongue to speak, a heart to bless?
These are *some* things, that will in fact,
  Make this great "Meeting" a success.

And next the "guests." No low-born race,
  Who lacked Ambition's sacred fire,
And ne'er aspired to higher place,
  Or made of *gain* their life's desire.

Again we ask—who, here to-day,
  Bid us to feast on "god"-ly food?
Who are the almoners who may
  Distribute for the "gods" our food?

Lawyers and Doctors, Preachers, stand
  As guard advanced, in war array;
While Teachers are no laggard band,
  Who keep dull ignorance at bay.

Diplomas writ in Latin text,
  Can sure be numbered by the score;
But what is good, and what comes next?
  Not one in mental gifts so poor,

But he may wield a scholar's pen,
Or sit in halls with learnéd men.
We're proud I say—and justly so,
For blood will "tell," where'er it go.

We're proud of ancestors and name,
  We glory in most worthy stock
  As staunch and true as Plymouth Rock,
We're proud as well, of deeds and fame.

Our Ancestors of whom we write,
　　Were men of *muscle*, as of *mind* ;
They wrought, and fought, with will and might,
　　In val'rous deeds were not behind.

" What's in a Name," we often hear,
　　Much that defines the owner's place,
And designates with index clear,
　　His claim to dignity and grace.

Our father's name—to us bequeathed,
　　Was never known to be disgraced
By meanness, or by vice enwreathed,
　　And *only marriage* has displaced.

This name, the " roll of honor " fills,
　　And they who bear it can lay claim
To poise, and strength of mind and will,
　　And many such are known to fame.

Honest in speech, to duty true,
Faithful to trust, whate'er they do,
Our hearts to-day swell high with pride,
That virtue leans to virtue's side.

Attraction and repulsion meet
　　As equal factors in their minds ;
Their love once given is no conceit,
　　But prejudice as strong, we find.

Abrupt and terse, though true as steel,
　　They often mar their friendships new ;
But yet—such *kindly hearts to feel*—
　　We sure would hide their faults from view.

Great worker—every Dickinson,
  For Dickinsons are all "true blue,"
They toil from rise to set of sun,
  And "paddles" each "his own canoe."

Our fathers' fathers, we are told,
  Both wrought, and studied, turn by turn;
Nor summer's heat, nor winter's cold,
  Could quench the ardent *wish to learn.*

Untrained in schools of modern kind,
  Unlearned in Science and in Art,
They yet were *better trained* in mind,
  And chose more oft, "the better part."

In many cases, as we learn,
  The Bible was the only Book
From which they drew those lessons stern,
  Which gave their lives such earnest look.

Their early training, gave them faith
  In "King James' version," *as it reads,*
And where it said—"And thus He saith,"
  That was their talisman of deeds.

No "new departure" shook belief
  In *lack of chances after death,*
Or gave to punishment relief
  From long continuance after breath,
Or held "rewards" as endless boon
  For *all*—no matter what their doom.

Their faith was simple, pure and bold,
  And Bible truth was truth indeed;
Their cheeks would blanch, their blood run cold,
  At modern changes in our creed.

Darwin and Huxley were unknown,
  Spencer and Mill were yet unborn;
Thank God they were! for these alone
  Would see our bark from moorings torn.

No doubting, scientific man,
  Spoke of the Bible with disdain;
God was His own interpreter,
  And He who wrote it made it plain.

In olden times those Bible men
Reared children many—often ten;
And oft the use of Bible *names*
Their love of Bible *lore* proclaims.

Nathan, Samuel, John, Nathaniel,
Thomas, Medad, Aaron, Daniel,
Elizabeth, Anna, Esther, Ruth,
Perez, Zebina, and in truth,
Such is the *host* of worthy names,
That time would fail to write their claims.

With all the gifts to Dickinsons,
They still are *innocent of one;*
Endowed with children, and with heirs.
The *dowry* mostly—*was in prayers.*

Whoever heard as "millionaired,"
The name of Dickinson declared?
There is among them no Rothschild
Grown rich by speculation wild.

They leave to Vanderbilt and Gould,
Jay Cooke and others of that mould,
To pocket millions by the bale,
And of huge railroads keep the tale.

MRS. CURRIER'S POEM.

Their purses shallow, small and thin,
  Open *too wide for others' needs*,
To keep much shining dust within,
  For gen'rous hearts do gen'rous deeds.

— ⋅⋅ —

Now having spoken thus at length
Upon our race and of its strength,
Let us before these words we close,
Speak just a word for some of those

Who labored for the highest good
Of all mankind, and who have stood
In many a dark and trying hour,
And vindicated manhood's power.

* * *

Of *Samuel Fowler*, Nathan's son,
A townsman here, in Amherst born;
We speak, of such as we've been told,
And hope the venture not too bold.

From Father, and from Mother, too,
The love of knowledge straight he drew;
So, youthful wish was gratified,
As with a College class he vied.

Old "Dartmouth" gave him his degree,
And second in his class was he;
To teaching, after, then he turned,
But for the *Law* his spirit yearned.

A Lawyer of no small repute,
  Cultured, and studious, honest, true;
His rank was high. Beyond dispute,
  A Saul for measure, in one view.

"Knowledge is power," he always taught,
And his own mind with Learning fraught,
Gave him an earnest strong desire
To kindle Learning's sacred fire.

As beacon-light on hill-top near,
Which guides and cheers the mariner,
His own fair town could boast no school
Where boys could *fit* for College rule.

As "wish is father to the thought,"
　　The *wish meant action* with that man,
Counsel and money then he sought,
　　And straight such school its life began.

With lengthened sight he saw the need
　　Of men with Education's skill,
To teach and preach on mission fields,
　　And mould the heathen mind at will.

So foll'wing out th' Apostle's word,
He "first gave *self* unto the Lord,"
And consecrated all his powers
To help and bless this world of ours.

And with himself—*an open hand*,
A steady purpose in command,
To build for God these College walls,
And train young men for Duty's calls.

His time, his infl'ence, and his prayers,
Despite his many worldly cares,
And all his gen'rous wealth, he gave
This College enterprise to save.

He sleeps beneath the churchyard green.
Which from this place is plainly seen;
The words upon his marble plain—
"A man though dead, shall live again."

But, should his epitaph be writ
   In lines of gold and heavenly blue,
We could not but this truth admit—
   "He builded better than he knew."

Many a preacher this day shares
This good man's wish—this good man's prayers;
But he, from down the "shining way"
Looks on well-pleased to see this day.

And we, who see this monument
Believe the wish from Heaven was sent
To do the right, and *build for God*,
Thus bless the world—at home—abroad.

"The *good* men do," the Poet says—
   "Is often with their bones interred,"
We mourn o'er these the worldly ways,
   But is it not sometimes *inferred?*
         *   *   *

Of *Edward*, Samuel's eldest son,
   An *honest Lawyer* like his sire,
We must one word before we're done,
   And hope your patience not to tire.

Knowledge was his, and legal skill,
Places of trust were his at will,
Where Right was Might, he mighty grew,
And proving wise, discreet and true.

The College gave him, it appears,
  Of College money—guardian care;
And not one cent in forty years,
  But had its record full and fair.

Once more, of this same eldest son,
  Such epitaph as this is best,
Which poet wrote, as benison,
  For faithful service long possessed:

    "Life's race well run,
    Life's work well done,
    Life's crown well won,
        And now—comes rest."

"Blessed are they who in the Lord
From labors rest, yea, saith the Word,
Their lives, their faith and hope proclaim,
And all their works do follow them."

—

'Tis said, "the actions of the just
Smell sweet and blossom in the dust."
The truth of this, who dare may doubt,
Who lifts his eyes and looks about?

A fragrant mem'ry left behind,
Of love to God and human kind,
In deeds of love *forgetting self,*
And every thought of worldly pelf,

Is like the rose, when twilight dews
Have quickened fragrance, and transfuse
A beauty born of shade and calm,
Like chastened sorrow's healing balm.

Thus, if we ever keep in mind,
That *joy in sacrifice we find*,
So shall we emulate the just,
Our motto this—"*In God we trust.*"
Aug. 8th, 1883.

THE PRESIDENT.—There might seem to be a little ambiguity with reference to the next announcement on the program—"That D- n Family and a Turn at Some Other Cranks," –a little doubt as to what it means. But after we have listened in the address to the allusions to the Deacons among the Dickinsons, I think there can be no doubt that this must be taken to mean "That Deacon Family, and a Turn at Some Other Cranks." We shall have the pleasure now of listening to an essay by Mr. Edward B. Dickinson, of New York, upon that subject.

In introducing his essay Mr. Dickinson said :

Brother Dickinson, and you who are his "sisters, and his cousins, and his aunts :" Although it has apparently gone hard with any Dickinson in the history of the family, who wore a red neck-tie (the speaker wearing one at the time) or who made puns, I still venture to express my gratification at standing for the first time in my life before an audience, so many of whom I can call by name, and yet so few of whom I know by sight. This reverses the usual order of things with me, as my infirmity has always been an inability to call by name a great many people whom I knew perfectly well by sight. From earliest childhood this has been my embarrassment. Why, when I was two months old, I knew my own mother perfectly well by sight, and yet I could not call her by name to save my uncut teeth.

When the funereal Secretary of the Committee notified me that I was the man selected to prepare and read an alleged humorous essay before the other members of the family, he very naturally wanted to know what it would be about. I told him that I thought it would be about half an hour; I also intimated to him that I thought somebody had assumed a very terrible responsibility in getting so many of the family together within the precincts of a hitherto quiet and inoffensive town, unless there was a substantial and commodious jail in which the family could be securely confined, so that when the spirit of mischief broke out, as it undoubtedly would, the family would be in a position where they could not break out. He admitted the hard impeachment, pleaded contributory negligence, and added to your already imminent peril by insisting that I should go on and prepare the eruption which will shortly break out among those of you who are rash enough to remain, after this warning.

With a view of ascertaining whether the essay could be read within the time allotted, I took the precaution on last Friday to catch my office boy————in mischief ————and to lock him into my inner office; and while he timed the performance, I read with much gesture and emphasis what I had written.

I deem it only fair to state, and I hope the Amherst papers will please copy,————that I understood that the funeral services of that office boy were to be held last Monday, at three o'clock P. M.

Mr. Dickinson then read an essay entitled:

THAT D——N FAMILY,

WITH A TURN AT SOME OTHER CRANKS.

Necessity knows no law; in which regard it is very like some of the Democratic Police Justices of the City of New York. Necessity is the mother of invention, and also of this Essay, which is a very patent invention born of ap-parent necessity. Necessity has been responsible, however, for many calamities besides the construction of this ebulition. One of which I wish to relate in order to better prepare you for the worse, which is to follow ; the sugar coating as it were of a bitter pill.

During the spring and summer of 1863, the Brigade of United States troops upon whose pay-rolls as the Adjutant General thereof I used to draw my pay with greater success than has attended my artistic efforts of drawing —————except perhaps, a cork————or to speak by the card, in rare moments of abstraction, drawing to three of a kind————was stationed in front of Port Hudson, La., trying like Tammany at a Democratic Convention to get in. The weather was terribly hot, and like the girl in the song, we "mopped the livelong day" ; in other words we were engaged in killing Louisiana Mosquitoes and confederate Musketeers.

The federal gun-boats had come up from wandering on the sea-beat shore, where they too had been "gathering shells" to "throw them one by one away" into Port Hudson. Those shells were no joke ; they never struck me as being at all funny ; indeed, I never heard of their striking any man, and his being at all funny afterwards. If you will bear in mind that the seats in this Hall are about 16 inches high, you will have some idea of the size of those 15 inch homeopathic globules of brotherly love which we used to exchange.

Many of these tributes of affection, striking in the soft, muddy soil, did not explode ; and great numbers of them were scattered around the place when at last it fell into our hands after a stubborn resistance by the confederates ; they had been compelled to eat their mules; and this absorption of mule meat into their systems was what made their resistance so stubborn and so tough generally.

The winter of 1863 was exceptionally severe, especially to the colored people accustomed to a warm climate,

One old man, probably a descendant of a good old nigger-bogger family of the South, whose Presidential name was Jefferson Madison Monroe, and who from his extreme age was supposed to have been the body servant of the father of the late lamented George W., and presumably the grandfather of his country, in the child-like innocense of his heart, had rolled with great labor one of the unexploded 15 inch shells into his little hut outside of the fortifications, and had buried it in his fire-place just half way up, the upper, dome-like half of the shell affording an excellent resting place for the tin sauce-pan in which he prepared his paté de foie gras. Colder and colder grew the weather; hotter and hotter grew the shell; and at the eleventh hour one unusually cold night, in the touching but enigmatical language of Mrs. Hemans:

"There came a burst of thunder sound,
The boy———Oh, where was he?"

This was a rebus that no fellow could find out. He left for parts unknown; and he also left a hole in the ground about 30 feet in diameter and what few chips he didn't have time to pass in. Some thought that this was a clear case of suicide, because the old boy didn't want to be buried in the ordinary graveyard, not being as he said, acquainted with the people living there; others thought that as he had become so accustomed to being blown up by people all his life, being blown up at the end of it would be to him a natural death.

Badly as I had known the colored people to be served, this was the first instance to my knowledge where one was served on the half shell.

The grave of the three Presidents, as this excavation was afterwards called, became the objective point of many a pleasure ride during the few months of inactivity preceding the Red River campaign. One eventful day, Col. H., of the Division Staff, desired to ride with a fair, dainty young creature, who had made sad havoc with the Colonel's martial heart. He had a thorough-bred horse which the lady was to ride, and he wanted one for himself. Now I had a horse, Joe Hooker by name, who was not a thorough-bred, but who was peculiar. And his peculiarity was in his gait; it might be called an eight-barred gate; it was so hard to get over. In trotting he came up very high behind, went down very low in front, and finished up with a spring of about two feet into the air, coming down with all four legs stiff upon the ground, with a shock calculated to fill his rider with unutterable surprise and profanity.

I had become accustomed to this peculiarity. He was a handsome, glossy beast, as steady under fire as a monument, standing nearly eighteen hands high; consequently I rode quite the high horse, and rather looked down on my brother patriots in Uncle Sam. Necessity compelled Col. H. to borrow my horse, ignorant or unmindful of anything but the sleek and glossy appearance of the animal. Equally unmindful of the consequences I acceded to the Colonel's request.

About three-quarters of an hour afterwards I saw the gallant Colonel and his lovely companion; she was radiant and rosy; he was red and wrathful; Joe Hooker, evidently entering into the spirit of the occasion, and desiring in his honest horse sense to make things lively for the young folks, was going up higher behind, coming down lower in front, jumping more and landing harder than I had ever known him to do before. The Colonel was evidently not entirely at his ease; he seemed to be having what has passed into classic English as "a parrot and monkey time." His pantaloons had "hitched up" nearly to his knees, as pantaloons will on such occasions unless strapped down or under top boots; his hat, a new one and a trifle too small, would not stay put, but at nearly every bounce came tilting down over the Colonel's nose. The Colonel's face wore a sad, dejected expression, as if he had suddenly been disappointed in love, or had unexpectedly encountered the business end of a bumble bee, and was prepared to say with the first of the Corinthian, "O, Death, where is *thy* sting?"

All things must have an end; even this Essay and tomorrow's excursion. So did this ride, born of necessity. And when the Colonel returned my horse, the language in which he indicated the "points" in that noble animal, was forcible, terse, but from a Sunday-school standpoint, quite incorrect.

This fable teaches us that nothing is so ungrateful as ingratitude; it may also serve to show how easy it is for a very small man to get used to riding a very large hobby; and how uncomfortable it makes the rest of the family if they have to ride it too.

To find an A. No. 1 subject for this Essay upon the lives of this distinguished family in this country cost me as much trouble as it cost the Government of Great Britain to find a "No. 1" subject supposed to have escaped to these Shores after an Essay upon the lives of a distinguished family in that country. Feeling that many of us do not care for essays when we can get pie, I picked out a pie for this feast of reason as just the dessert you would like to get; but knowing that most of us do not like to get our just desert until as late a date as possible,—prefer to make a post mortem affair of it if we can,—and not being a Coroner in quest of an inquest,—I desert pie as being a possible source of crustiness and disagreement.

Soap bubbled up suggestively. This had much to recommend it; the universality of the subject, "where there's life, there's soap." The fondness of the Dickinson Nation for soap————soft soap; its ancient origin, found as it is in all times and in all tongues, and on most of the picturesque rocks and board fences along the line of the Pennsylvania Railroad, ———— ——I even found a small piece once in Pittsburgh ; the ease with which it is applied ; its miraculous power of transformation into the antique of a freshly painted human ruin ; the theological aspect of soap; cleanliness being akin to godliness, and there being no cleanliness without soap. But not wishing to be soporific, I have resolutely abstained from its use during this trip.

Whales, too, came to the surface ; I thought as it were to seize my subject from the seas. Whales suggest sea voyages ; and sea voyages suggest sea-sickness ; which after all is the greatest test of the value of a friend ; we often never would have supposed there was so much *in* a man, until we had been to sea.

Besides, one should always know something about his subject. I know all about whales ; I have often been whaled. Although my father did not pursue that exciting branch of our industrial tree for an honest livelihood, I have known the exciting branch of a tree to industriously pursue me ; and for a real honest, lively wood ————in the quaint, sad language of Wall Street, "That yanks the bakery." My father was very successful as a whaler; his whaling trips were frequent, and productive of unlimited blubber; it came literally in tears. We were both in the business ; he did the whaling, and I attended to the wailing. Between us both those were indeed squally times.

But whales are great blowers : and being a Dickinson I am naturally opposed to rivalry in my own line ; so I abstain from lampooning the whale ; again it will be a large subject to handle, and I doubt if I could handle a full grown one successfully. Moreover, I have always associated whales with Job ; Job, not Jonah. I never associated much with Jonah, except that one swallow did not make him spring. Job became the bright and shining light of other days through the instrumentality of severe boils. And whales became the bright and shining light of other days through the instrumentality of severe boiling. And in both cases, trying as the process was, it seemed to turn out "oil for the best."

Noses also turned up as an elevating subject; we have some of us taken as many as 33 degrees of elevation in that regard; the royal arch, in fact. I know how it is myself; it is the only prominence I ever expect to achieve. It occurred to me that I ought to try and hit off some of the family characteristics. Though not usually pug-*n*osious, some of us who have full blown noses might resent having them hit off. Nothing demands more careful attention, especially during a cold wave, than our respective noses; still we like to have them handled tenderly even by members of our own family. In giving a parting pull at the nose, I may add that it is well that in the human face, as in a motion to adjourn in hot weather, the eyes and nose are usually two to one. Most of us, I hope, are too wise to lay claim to more than one nose. Except on the hypothesis that the Dickinsons are all up to snuff, which is possibly the case————one 's nough. And sometimes one is more than enough; the nose, as it is the head centre of humanity, is usually found in the middle of the face; some noses, however, are found in the middle of other people's business; where they are clearly out of place, not to say out of joint. We most of us have suffered from finding somebody else's nose in some phase of our affairs; which is only another illustration of the unpleasantness of two noses in the same face.

After much reflection I decided upon the subject as it stands printed on the program, which you have all seen. I was sorry to hear from the mournful Secretary that while he liked the subject,————from which I infer that he meant the family, and expected a gentle turn with the other cranks,————he was afraid that the many reverend gentlemen who were to be present would supply the wrong letters to the long dash. This seemed to indicate a conviction on his part that the irresistible tendency of the clerical mind is toward profanity.

I hope that I shall treat the august subject of this essay,——————for owing to the month it is really an August subject,—————with considerable generosity, as it undoubtedly will require considerable generosity to treat so large a crowd to anything but water; and one cannot expect much water in so dry a thing as an essay on this Eastern Union; this Dickinson stock has never been watered; there has been so little Gofu)ld in the family.

To give one good turn to all the family cranks will require time, as one good turn deserves another; and the family has always been the crankiest thing one can know; except one canoe which I once had, made of birch bark: But that canoe was very easily upset, especially when full. Nothing can upset a Dickinson, no matter how full he is.

To properly account for the original Dickinsons,—————and the Dickinsons are all more or less original,—————I subdivide this tale into heads: The origin, the rise, the peculiarities, and the decline of the tribe.

The origin of a Dickinson is lost in the obscurity of the Middle Ages; this may account for the obscurity of many a middle aged Dickinson like myself. And it may occur to the natives of Amherst that it would not have been wholly a disaster if the original Dickinson had also been lost in the obscurity of the Middle Ages. I looked in vain for the Genesis of the family in the book of Genesis, but I found no allusion to them in the history of the creation. It would have been a step of doubtful expediency to project a full grown Dickinson into a new, young and inexperienced world, such as it was before the deluge. It would have doubtless precipitated that remarkable rainfall some hundreds of years. I am convinced, therefore, that there were no Dickinsons in the time of Noah, as I find no record of any in Noah's Archives. If there had been one at that time, he would surely have been on board the Ark, as there never was a Dickinson yet who didn't know enough to go in when it rained. And if he had gone in he would have run the Ark, or there would not have been e'er-a-rat at the termination of the voyage.

Again, all the other animals went into the Ark two and two, each after his kind, and there never have been two of a kind in the family. I conclude that the only authentic *Noah* Dickinson is of later date, and is not located in Asia Minor, but in Amherst.

The Reverend gentleman who preceded me gave an account of many Dickinsons who have gained wholesale credit in great store for the family. This is especially gratifying, as I know that some of us have not always been able to get credit, even in a retail store. He has also relieved our minds of great uncertainty, by telling us where we all came from. I regret that he did not relieve our minds of a still greater uncertainty by telling us where we are all going to.

Having successfully failed to account for the origin of the family, I am compelled to admit his statements as authentic, barring some natural clerical mistakes. The origin itself was a mistake, I think. And the only hypothesis upon which I can explain it, is the predestined destruction of my native State of Massachusetts, on the scientific theory of natural selection, and the non-survival of the fittest, as foreshadowed in the natural selection of that State as the fittest receptacle into which to pour this double distilled extract of all the Dickinsons, and the dead certainty which exists in my mind of the non-survival of Massachusetts.

The rise of the family has been very slow; such members of it as I know have been very reluctant to rise at all, and never got up until the second bell rang. The heaviest sleeper I ever saw was a near relative of mine. I don't like to say how much he did weigh; but it was a very long way, for it took two hay scales to weigh him, and then one had to weight; and he was not hay-scaly fellow at all. He was so heavy a sleeper that he broke through the floor one night and fell through the china closet into the kitchen. He would have fallen into China only the range broke his fall. It also broke his leg, and would doubtless have broken his neck, only the Dickinsons are such a stiff-necked generation that they never get all broken up. One doctor set his leg, but it required four masons to set the range ready for the next fall. We moved him over the soft water cistern, as the water, being soft, would not hurt him. There are also several others, I think, whom soft water would not hurt.

Natural aptitude and industry, coupled with perseverance, have often sent a man up under the fostering care of the free institutions of the land, with surprising rapidity. I know of one man whose natural aptitude and industry, coupled with a pen, sent him up for ten years in about twenty minutes. Under the fostering care of a free institution of the land at Sing Sing, he was made a blacksmith on account of his familiarity with the forge.

In the new Directory of the great City of New York there are only forty-four Dickinsons all told. I learn with amazement that in the little town of Amherst there are forty-two Dickinson voters. With all its fortitude I know now why Amherst has not grown to be as large as New York. The forty-two Dickinsons, like large numbers of other daisies in pasture lands, have absorbed all the richness of the soil and choked out other forms of vegetation. When Goldsmith described the Deserted Village he must have had the village of Amherst in mind, when he says :

"Amazed the gazing rustics ranged around ;
And still they gazed, and still the wonder grew,
That one small town could carry all that crew."

Goldsmith never wrote quite so full of feeling, and probably never was feeling quite so full, as when he wrote that.

Of the forty-four Dickinsons in the New York Directory, there are but two laborers,———which speaks ill for our industry ; seven widows, which speaks well for our endurance ; and one car conductor, which speaks volumes for the bell punch. Forty-three of the forty-four are probably more or less dissatisfied with their respective occupations, as all of us are apt to be at times. The exception to this rule, one whose name is printed in capital letters, is a chimney sweep. His occupation has always sooted him.

Having thus taken the rise out of the family, I pass on to their peculiarities. One of our boasted peculiarities is strength of will. We call it firmness, others occasionally call it pig-headedness. It is sometimes said that the Dickinson will was never broken. I think that is over-confidence. Let any one of you attempt to bequeath the property you leave behind you, in any eccentric or unexpected manner, and see how quick the girl you leave behind you will break your will,——— as is the wont of disappointed families, in which case the family wont will prove stronger than the individual will.

Together with much will we have great personal pride, and much personal vanity, especially among the men. Strange to say this peculiarity seems to lead us to indulge in periods of protracted reflection. I have often seen a full grown, well looking male Dickinson, absorbed in apparently the most satisfactory reflections.——— ——— from a full length looking-glass. The only exception to this, so far as my own reflection teaches me, arises from a curious obliquity of vision, caused by too much looking in glasses, whereby we see double. This wounds our vanity to find that any two others can be exactly like us and besides, nobody likes, upon due reflection, to be unexpectedly doubled up.

After my previous statements it is needless to say that we are a very truthful family, especially when talking about other people. From the oldest to the youngest we all tell the truth ; and the younger we get, the more of it we tell. I met a man whom I was proud to know belonged to us. He was never heard to utter an untruth ; nor was he ever heard to say an unkind word of any one ; moreover, he could never hear disparaging remarks concerning others, uttered in his presence. He shed a brilliant lustre on our name. He was deaf and dumb.

We are also a courageous family ; full of pluck ; lots of grit. I was apprehensive that being so full of pluck and having so much grit, that we might set to and pluck each other if anything particularly gritty was said. My apprehensions were allayed by remembering that in all the family jars I ever got into————except when I got into the family preserve jars————it all ended in talk. In such conflicts discussion seems to be the better part of valor.

We are generous ; generous to a fault ; particularly to our own faults. We are also inclined to be extravagant, consequently we find it sometimes difficult to live within our incomes. My difficulty has not been in living within an income, but in living without one. It is strange that some of us have not invested more extensively in the poultry business ; we have such a wonderful facility for turning our money into ducks and drakes.

While being generous and even extravagant, we are singularly averse to hospitality. So marked is this aversion to hospitality that no matter how sick we are, we are never willing to be sent to a hospital. Not a single member of the family would ever permit himself to be sent to one, even as a last resort. Some of us who are not single are occasionally glad to be sent almost anywhere as a last resort, without a permit.

Our hates and our loves are very pronounced ; that is to say, we do not hesitate to speak about them. Our hatred of snakes, for instance, amounts to actual delirium, especially when we fancy we have them in our boots. Our attachments are equally strong. I once had an extremely ferocious dog which had settled the outstanding accounts of several creditors who were also standing out, by devouring them. The dog was not mad, but quite a number of trades people were, however. I valued him as a keepsake————a sort of memento mori. One of our distant relatives————very distant in fact; he lived in Australia————came to visit us. He was very fond of dogs, and became very firmly attached to this one————by the seat of his trousers; an attachment which was only vacated when he vacated the trousers, which he did at a cost of about half a yard of very raw material. He said he didn't mind this vacation of his trousers so much, because they were his vacation trousers. He walked to his hotel in a barrel, and took his meals off the mantelpiece for a month afterwards. The dog had only been true to the family principle : to cling to those who were fond of him.

We are all of us ambitious and aspiring ; from earliest childhood we yearn for wealth, for fame, for position. The passing years bring to most of us no change. As we grow older still we (y)earn————our living.

Having enlarged upon many of our peculiarities, and having invented such as I could not enlarge, you will observe that in doing so I have devoted attention to the masculine attributes of our family, in this treatise. However great this treat is to them, it would be a greater treat to me to be permitted to pay devoted attention to the feminine element. For obvious reasons I have felt that I could not to-day more than just begin to do so in half an hour. To-morrow I trust the elements will allow me to remedy this omission, and it will be in accord with my invariable rule————never to do to-day that which I am obliged to put off until to-morrow.

I never was fortunate enough to have a sister; although I did get somebody else's sister to have me. In my own particular branch of the Dickinsons the children are all boys. For generations we have not run much to girls in our family; but we have made up for it by running a good deal after the girls in other families. Having always been a bashful and retiring man, and having little experience with the gentler sex, I am unable to talk much about the feminine element in the family. But I do not think it necessary; what little experience I have had has taught me that when occasion offers they can talk for themselves. That is, I presume they must talk for themselves; as whenever eight or ten of them get together it never has seemed to me that any one of them had time to listen to anything except what she was saying herself. It was always a sort of a go-as-you-please affair; and every one of them kept going without any lapse.

After to-morrow's permanent organization the family is likely to sink into a slow decline. I judge so, because we have always been slow to decline anything so permanently organized as to be wholly ours————except the smallpox. The only man I ever knew who seemed really glad to get the smallpox permanently into his organization was a well-known public man, many years ago, whose life was made a burden to him by the crowd of office seekers asking for all sorts of things. He said he was glad that he had got something at last that he could give to everybody who came to him. With all our generosity, few of us are for-giving to that extent.

The most remarkable instance of a slow decline in the

family occurred when I used to be called upon to decline an irregular Greek verb. I always sank into a very slow decline. If I had my choice I should have much prefered to decline half a dozen regular whippings than one irregular verb.

Having come about to the end of my rope————an unique distinction, as I believe no Dickinson has ever yet come to the end of a rope————it remains for me to express my regret that I shall probably never again have an opportunity to get all the members of my family together by the ears as I have done during this reading ————a fact which you are likely to regard in the light of a special providence————I desire to close this essay by another essay to correct a slight loss of gravity, which I fancied I observed at certain stages of this journey. Many stages have been completely overturned through a disregard of the constant operations of the law of gravity.

To prepare you for the loftier flight of the poet who is to follow me————Oh, my prophetic soul, my uncle ————I too soar into poetry, knowing no better way to prepare you for flight; and after the old custom of throwing old shoes for luck after parting friends, I fling to you these under stanzas, which I hope you will understand, Sirs, as a parting fling; I call it "Old Shoes"— some old shoes, containing my *last* puns:—

> "How much we all are like old shoes;
> For instance; we both a soul may lose;
> Both have been tanned; both are made tight
> By cobblers; both get left, and right;
> Both need a mate to be complete,
> And both are made to go on feet.
> We both need heeling, oft are soled,
> And both in time turn all to mould.

With shoes the last is first ; with men
The first shall be the last ; and when
The shoes wear out, they're mended new ;
When we wear out, we are men dead, too.
We both are trod upon, and both
Will tread on others, nothing loath.
Both have our ties, and both incline,
When polished, in the world to shine.
And both peg out ; which would you choose ?
To be yourselves————or to be your shoes ?
                                       (Applause).

The President —I have now to present Gideon Dickinson, M. D., of Milford, who will read a poem.

Dr. Dickinson then read the following poem :

THE EXILES.

PROEM.

Dear friends, and kindred by the father's side,
And ye who are maternally allied ;
Mothers and daughters, every sire and son,
(I'll not forget or willingly slight one,)
For it would grieve my heart to thrust aside
Even those but matrimonially allied ;
Nor could I, if I would, for marriage ties
Are stronger than they seem to unskilled eyes ;
What do I hear you say ? Did some one speak ?
Affirming that the marriage tie is weak ?
Let the deluded fool, who would forsake
"His better half," but once attempt to break
That "silken tie," and he shall find it strong,—
It firmly binds unwilling hearts too long !
But this, indeed, is neither "here nor there,"
A slight digression, made to shield "the fair,"

"The fair," whose graceful charms our hearts enslave,
"The fair," designed by nature for the brave.
But to return: some friends oft wrote to me
To say a mighty gathering there would be
Of all our kindred from both far and near,
And very kindly urged me to be here.
Well, that, unto myself I quickly said,
Will be right pleasant, for we shall be fed
With the rich dainties from our kinsmens' store,
And feast on luxuries ne'er known before;
Believing, child-like, that, invited here,
We should feast fair upon their royal cheer;
I took it all for granted, and could see
A grand symposium, made for you and me;
"A feast of reason and a flow of soul,"
With loaded plate and overflowing bowl;
Where we, sad wanderers from the ancestral home—
Like "Ilium's remnant," long compelled to roam—
Called back to the ancestral halls, at last,
Amid the memories of the mighty past,
Should, round the ancestral hearth-stone feast and laugh,
And, for us, should be killed the fatted calf;
And we should meet to feast and drink our fill;
While some one else should kindly—pay the bill!
A feast of reason, with no angry flaw,
Backed by the Church[1] and shielded by the Law.[2]
But ah, alas! each pleasure hath its pain;
And, when I read their letters o'er again,
I noticed, with a tremor of affright,
Some unread lines, wherein they bade me write
A poem for the occasion, where should shine
The glories of our clan, in lofty rhyme;
A grand high-sounding poem, some such thing
As minstrels—in old times—were wont to sing;

---

[1] The orator of the day was an eminent clergyman.
[2] The chairman of the meeting was a distinguished lawyer.

Recounting the brave deeds of former times,
Sung, to their tuneful harps, in rugged rhymes;
And so, I've journeyed far, through dust and heat,
By them invited, here with you to meet;
And, at their bidding, I will read you here
My humble rhymes, and then we'll taste their cheer.
But all I yet have said is but the proem
To what is yet to come, that is, my poem;
No lofty epic, claiming tears and smiles,
But the sad story of Some Poor Exiles.

I

In a far clime, beyond the stormy ocean,
   Ages ago there dwelt a hardy race,
That, boldly mingling in the world's commotion,
   Confronted danger with undaunted face.

II.

Ah! those far days were days of doubt and trial,
   Dark days that deeply tried the souls of men,
Days of stern deeds and hardy self-denial;
   When shall we look upon their like again?

III.

In those dark days, a race of heroes, rising,
   Avowed the freedom of the human mind;
And, all the power of tyranny despising,
   Prepared to strike for God, and home, and kind.

IV.

Their stern and manly deeds, on history's pages,
   Adorn the records of their native soil,
And teach the lesson, to all coming ages,
   That freedom must be won with blood and toil.

V.

Some unborn Virgil yet shall sing their story,
  And weave their noble deeds in lofty rhyme,
And crown their names with bright, unfading glory,
  To point a moral for all coming time.

VI.

There woman, with a bearing sweet and lowly,
  Of every danger quick to share a part,
Inspiring all with trust both high and holy,
  Winning and sharing love with her pure heart;

VII.

Oh, where and when was ever human sorrow
  That God's best angel, woman, did not share?
And man's proud heart from her sweet love must borrow
  The comfort, strength and trust found only there;

VIII.

Yes, noble woman, hoping, trusting ever,
  Shrank not to share the perils of the sea;
To bid adieu to home and friends forever,
  The loved of earth she never more might see.

IX.

England's green fields were fair and bright around them,
  And God's great sun shone on them from above,
But tyranny and stern oppression bound them
  And bade them fly from scenes of home and love.

X.

As that brave band, when Ilium sank and perished,
  Amid the ruin, never stooped to fear,
But left the spot, on earth, most dearly cherished
  And fled from ruined homes once loved and dear.

XI.

So our brave exiles, bowed by stern oppression,
    Launched their frail barks upon an unknown sea:
Shrank not to leave inherited possession
    And dare all dangers, so they might be free.

XII.

And noble woman, with a patient bearing,
    Met suffering and hardship without fear;
Heroically, too, all dangers sharing,
    Hiding, with mild-eyed patience, many a tear.

XIII.

And, with brave words and love, faint hearts sustaining,
    While flying from the homes they loved so well,
Heroically bearing, uncomplaining,
    Dangers and sorrows, more than tongue can tell.

XIV.

Thus, with brave hearts, but sad, upon the ocean
    They launch their barks where stormy billows swell,
And with bowed souls, bursting, with deep emotion,
    To friends and home sigh out this long farewell:—

1.

    Farewell, farewell to childhood's home!
        Farewell to friends most dear!
    By tyranny compelled to roam,
        We go with sigh and tear.

2.

    We spread our sails to raging winds,
        And dare a stormy sea,
    Because oppression chains our minds
        And, here, we are not free.

3.

We fly from homes we dearly love,
  From early homes and friends,
And put our trust in God above,
  To take what fate He sends.

4.

Oh, may the stormy sea prove kind!
  Kinder than tyrants are;
May He, who rules both sea and wind,
  Still hold us in His care.

5.

Yon brazen sun, with angry frown,
  Sinks in the western sea;
Our bark with him may yet go down,
  And we all buried be.

6.

And if it should,—God's will be done!
  We still will trust His love;
And, when our earthly course is run,
  May we all meet above.

7.

Our native hills and vales, so dear,
  We leave with sorrowing heart;
And from our friends, and kindred near,
  'Tis bitterness to part.

8.

But who can live 'neath tyrants' thrall?
  Tyrants who chain the mind;
Better, by far, risk life and all
  That freedom we may find.

9.

Oh, earthly ties are hard to break
  Which bind to home and friends!
But friends and home we now forsake
  To take what fate God sends.

10.

Oh, may He guard those left behind!
  And us, in safety, keep!
To His bright throne our trust we bind
  And dare the raging deep.

11.

The pain it costs to part from home,
  No human tongue can tell:
By tyranny compelled to roam,
  Dear friends and home Farewell!

XV.

Now, far upon the trackless waste of ocean,
  Our dauntless exiles hold their weary course;
For days and weeks, the sea, in wild commotion,
  Beats on their straining bark with mighty force.

XVI.

Till, worn by weeks of toil, with eyes o'erflowing,
  They hail, with joyous hearts, the distant land;
Where the white breakers, in the red light glowing,
  Beat, with wild fury, on a desert strand.

XVII.

Rough winds and breakers gave them a rude greeting
  As their worn bark drew to New England's shore,
Where trackless forests ever were repeating
  The Indian's war-whoop and the wild beast's roar.

XVIII.

They came not with a conqueror's assurance
  To take possession of a favored land;
But, with strong arms and hearts of brave endurance,
  They came a weary, worn, God-fearing band.

XIX.

Hard were their toils, replete with self-denials,
  While, with brave hearts, they built New England homes;
With countless years of danger, and deep trials,
  They built, for us, fair towns and towering domes.

XX.

With blood and toil they founded our great nation,
  As ancient heroes founded mighty Rome;
Each one, a hero in his proper station,
  Suffered and toiled for country and for home.

XXI.

Fast rolling years are weaving doubt and mystery
  Round the dim records of that far-off time.
Then, quickly, may the mighty pen of history,
  In golden letters, write their deeds sublime.

XXII.

Let Boston guard her founders' graves with honor,
  And carve their shining names upon her gates![1]
Those names have shed immortal fame upon her,
  And stand with those who founded mighty States.

---

1. In 1882 the City of Boston, through her constituted authorities, ordered "Memorial Tablets" to be prepared and placed upon the gates of the old cemeteries on Tremont street. The tablets are in bronze, and bear the names of John Winthrop, 1620; John Leveret, 1679; John Cotton, 1652; John Davenport, 1670; Jacob Sheafe, 1658; John Winslow, 1674; Mary Clinton, 1679, a passenger in the Mayflower, and wife of John Winslow; with many other of the distinguished names of Boston's early settlers and founders.

XXIII.

Their deeds adorn their country's noble story,
   And gild with glory many a hard-fought field ;
Let ages yet to come repeat their story,
   And to their noble names due honors yield.

XXIV.

They shine on Bancroft's grand, historic pages,
   They ring, harmonious, in the poet's song,
And stand a beacon-light, to coming ages,
   To blast oppressors and oppressive wrong.

XXV.

They won for us the greatest of all treasures,
   A noble country free from tyrant's thrall ;
New England homes, with all their untold pleasures,
   Free from dark Superstition's damning pall.

XXVI.

To one bold patriot of those gloomy ages
   Our thoughts, to-day, especially we turn ;
And write his honored name within our pages
   And weave one chaplet for his crumbling urn.[1]

XXVII.

To him, and his compatriots, all honor
   And the deep tribute of the heart we give ;
And dear New England, may God smile upon her,
   Through their brave deeds, her name shall ever live.

XXVIII.

Yes, dear New England! freedom, peace and gladness
   Reign in thy happy homes and pleasant dells ;

---

1. Nathaniel Dickinson, one of the original settlers in the old town of Hadley, Mass.; the first of the name to come to this country, where he settled 223 years ago.

And, on thy holy Sabbath, never sadness,
  Or moan, is heard in thy sweet Sabbath-bells :—

1.

New England's bells—her Sabbath-bells—
  Proclaim New England's joy and peace ;
And all their tones, in happy homes,
  From toil and care sound sweet release.

2.

Those Sabbath-bells, their music tells
  Of freedom, peace and holy prayer ;
And no sad moans, with their sweet tones,
  Are wafted on the peaceful air.

3.

I've heard sweet chimes in foreign climes—
  In foreign climes beyond the sea—
But never chimes, in other climes,
  Could sound so joyously and free.

4.

New England's hills, and vales and rills,
  Where dwell the brave and fair and free !
When e'er I roam, far, far from home,
  Their joyous memory goes with me.

5.

Oh, many a time, in foreign clime,
  Where only human thought is free,
My blood would boil, to see the toil
  Of men bowed down by tyranny.

6.

There men like slaves go to their graves,
  And millions die that few may thrive ;

And mothers pale, to hush the wail
    Of starving children vainly strive.

7.

And childhood dear, with sigh and tear,
    Contends with gaunt-eyed misery;
While titled pride in coach doth ride,
    And rules with rod of tyranny:

8.

And maidens fair, with beauty rare,
    Are bowed to sin by dire distress;
While Cross and Creed to fatness feed
    And swell, with pomp, in silken dress.

9.

God bless our clime, and every chime
    Rung out to tell of freedom won!
Till round the world those chimes are hurled,
    Through every clime beneath the sun.

10.

O, Sabbath bells! your music tells
    Of sweet repose, and peace and prayer;
But from the domes, mid foreign homes,
    Sad, wailing chimes break on the air.

11.

New England's hills and vales and rills—
    God bless them in all coming time!
Her Sabbath-bells—her sunny dells—
    God's blessing on our happy clime.

12.

I've heard bells chime in many a clime—
    In many a clime beyond the sea—

But in their tones were half-heard moans,
 Which made their chimes sad chimes—for me.

XXIX.

God's blessing on New England's hills and valleys,
 Where peace and plenty smile in Freedom's arms;
Where, far and wide, men walk the sun-lit alleys
 Free from dark tyranny or war's alarms.

XXX.

Oh, may each heart, with gratitude o'erflowing,
 Bend o'er the grave of every patriot-sire
Who early toiled to set the flame a-glowing
 Which blazed to light the world with Freedom's fire.

XXXI.

Turn back Time's leaves two hundred years—
 Two hundred years and more—
And see what on that page appears,
 And view it o'er and o'er.
Then might you see these hill-tops fair
 With virgin forests crowned;
And in these valleys, everywhere,
 Reigned silence most profound,
Save where primeval forests bend
 Before the freshening breeze;
Or when the birds of Summer send
 Their songs from green-wood trees;
Or if the stealthy red-man steals
 Through dark ravines, below,
His sudden shout, at times, reveals
 His triumph o'er a foe.
No busy wheels, in valleys fair,
 Were turned by rushing stream.

And never, on the startled air,
  Was heard the steam-horse' scream.
Our fathers came, a feeble band—
  A wilderness was here—
But, with brave heart and willing hand,
  Dangers soon disappear.

XXXII.

Pause we here, to gaze with sadness
  Down the corridors of time ;
Hear we not the fathers' voices,
  While we tell their deeds sublime ?
See we not the waving forests,
  Where the stealthy red men creep ?
See we not the smoking hamlet,
  Where the doomed are roused from sleep ?
Yes ; but bravely our forefathers
  Seize the ready pike and gun ;
Soon the savage red men vanish—
  Freedom's work is well begun !
How they toiled, and how they suffered,
  None, to-day, can truly know ;
But we reap the ripened harvest
  Which their hands, with toil, did sow.
Let us love them for the blessings
  They, for us, prepared with care ;
Which the oppressed, of every nation,
  Freely come with us, to share.
By their deeds they taught the lesson,
  Which, to all the world may show,
That whoever would have freedom,
  He himself must strike the blow.

XXXIII.

But why should I the strain prolong,
  Which falls upon a wearied ear ?

Or lengthen out a closing song,
    Which few, perchance, will care to hear?
Those times are changed, those heroes gone,
    But one who bears their honored name
May love to weave an idle song
    Of olden times and deeds of fame,
When sterling worth was not despised,
    Though clothed in garb of ancient make,
And manly deeds were justly prized
    And duly praised for manhood's sake.
And fain would I, to ladies fair,
    Recount the woes our fathers bore,
And sing the virtues, sweet and rare,
    Of noble dames in days of yore:
Valor and worth then oft combined
    Where only simple garbs were seen,
And the rich virtues of the mind
    Were borne with meek and modest mien;
Then noble souls, in life's brief span,
    Could walk the earth with humble ways—
Nine tailors never made a man!
    There were no dudes in those brave days!
Then sterling valor, worth, and truth
    Were sure to win and wear the prize;
No hope was there for callow youth—
    They held no place in ladies' eyes;
Then maids were fair, and men were brave!
    And vanity dared not intrude;
Then youth, to age due reverence gave,
    And no one knew the brainless dude.

XXXIV.

But why should I still linger in my song?
    The hour has struck which tells me we must part;
Then why, at will, an idle strain prolong,
    Whose feeble notes may fail to reach the heart?

And if, at some sad strain, one tear should start,
   Beauty's bright smile will chase that tear away;
And passing sigh leave never painful smart,
   To tinge the pleasure of succeeding day;
   But tear and sigh will pass, and beauty will decay.

XXXV.

But ere I quit the theme which strung my lyre,
   I fain would sound one closing note for those
Who boldly lighted Freedom's blessed fire,
   Which banished from our land men's darkest woes;
Oh, may that blessed flame consume all foes
   Who seek to chain the forms and souls of men!
Till Tyranny shall sink in death's dark throes,
   And Bigotry flee howling to his den;
   Our sires' departed shades may smile upon us then

XXXVI.

Now unto all who listen to my song
   Be the deep thanks of an o'erflowing heart;
The winged hours, that swiftly sweep along,
   Already mark the moment when we part;
   But never from the singer's feeling heart
Shall pass the memory of this happy day;
   And when dark sorrows force a tear to start,
Thoughts of this hour shall chase that tear away;
And kindest wish for you shall only with him stay.

XXXVII.

The song shall cease, the harp shall be unstrung;
   Its echoes ne'er again may greet your ears,
Save when some spirit-tone its chords have rung
   Shall faintly echo down the coming years.
If any here then walk this vale of tears,
   Upon some breaking heart that tone may fall;

And, from the tomb of the long-buried years,
　That spirit-note some memory shall recall,
　To soothe a sinking soul, which bids adieu to all.

XXXVIII.

Now, unto you the minstrel sighs farewell!
　Nor heeds the sorrow of his own sad heart;
Yet, more than words of song can truly tell,
　He deeply feels the pain it costs to part;
　But if, in Beauty's eye, one tear shall start,
Responsive to some strain his harp hath rung,
　Then not in vain he tried the minstrel-art—
Not all in vain his feeble lips have sung—
For Beauty's grateful tear is dear to old and young.

XXXIX.

Yet once again, farewell! farewell to all!
　Too late we met, and all too soon we part.
The minstrel's song may cease in bower and hall,
　But tones of love shall linger in the heart:
And when, in some dark hour, a tear shall start,
　Thoughts of your love shall dry that tear again;
And green-eyed Censure, with his poisoned dart,
　May seek to wound the minstrel's heart in vain,
If, saying now farewell, we e'er may meet again.

THE PRESIDENT—If the audience will remain seated a moment I will make an announcement. I think that we shall be obliged to suspend the literary exercises until after dinner.

The photographer desires to take a photograph of the family, and has fixed the hour at three o'clock this afternoon; it is desirable that all should be present at that time, in front of this building, to have the photograph taken. After adjourning for dinner, we will return here and finish the exercises.

I wish to request all to record their names in the book which the Secretary has in the vestibule. Every person who has any Dickinson blood in his veins is requested to record his or her name.

I want to make one more important announcement. There is to be a reception in this hall this evening at 7:30 o'clock. It will be a very pleasant occasion; we shall have an opportunity of seeing each other socially, and I hope everyone will be here. I have taken the liberty of asking a few of the ladies and gentlemen to assist in the reception. We want somebody to be present,—a few persons to receive those who may come, and introduce friends to the Reception Committee.

Prof. Chevreaux has sent an invitation to the members of the family to visit his institution. I cannot announce what they are doing from hour to hour, but some of the exercises will be going on at each hour of the day at the college building. I have in my hand the program of this college, which may be distributed to any who desire to have it.

After the collation, the members of the family assembled in front of the College Hall in a group, and were photographed by Mr. Lovell, of Amherst.

AFTERNOON SESSION, WEDNESDAY, AUGUST 8TH,
THREE O'CLOCK P. M.

THE PRESIDENT—Reference has been made to the fact that a large number of our family are connected with the Society of Friends, so numerous in Pennsylvania. We have with us to-day, a very distinguished member of our family—a gentleman who is at the head of the Medical Society of the State of Pennsylvania, whose home is at Plymouth Meeting, in that State. I have the pleasure of introducing to you Doctor Hiram Corson.

Dr. Corson spoke as follows:

Ladies and Gentlemen—It is with some emotion, caused by the honor conferred upon me, for which I am very thankful, that I stand here; I can only say that I do not expect to address you, and I hope that you will excuse me; I made no preparation to address you. I feel in the presence of this audience gathered together to do honor to the long line of ancestors, coming down from Old England, and at every stage and period of their time, honoring their ancestry,—I feel that this should inspire me to make a proper response to your invitation. But, as I said before, I do not expect to address you; and if I were to address you at all, it would be that I might pay a tribute to our common founder. It is only ten years, perhaps, since I paid any attention to the genealogy of my mother's family, and I was quite ignorant of this great settlement of Dickinsons throughout Massachusetts, and of that great settlement of Dickinsons in Virginia, Maryland and New Jersey. I found, in looking at the references with my friend, Wharton Dickinson, year after year, with the others of this family, and at the very top of the Dickinson ancestry, we see the name of John Dickinson. It is from that source that we trace our origin. And yet there are eight generations from that John Dickinson before it reaches me. And there are two generations here to-day, down below me of that line.

I have been interdicted, I might say, almost by a promise, certainly by self-preservation, from addressing you further. Wharton Dickinson can tell you all that is necessary better than I can, of the line from which himself and I descended. And I beg you to excuse me from further addressing you.

THE PRESIDENT It gives me pleasure to introduce a gentleman who has been referred to by the last speaker —a gentleman who has given a great deal of attention to family genealogies in his own state, and I have no doubt he can instruct us very greatly. I take pleasure in introducing Mr. Wharton Dickinson, of Scranton, Pennsylvania.

Mr. Wharton Dickinson then addressed the audience, as follows:

Six hundred people, all claiming kinship (and what is still more remakable, proving it by certain distinctive features), assembled together in one place, is no ordinary spectacle. Judges and Generals, Senators and Colonels, Reverends and Doctors, Lawyers and Editors, Poets and Artists, Merchants and Bankers, Farmers and Mechanics, Young Men and Maidens, Old Men and Women, all met together to do reverence and esteem to the name and memory of the man and women, to whom all present, of the Dickinson blood, owe a common existence. What a theme for the pen of a poet, or the brush of a painter! Deeply do I feel the honor your committee have conferred upon me, in according me the privilege of addressing you on this august occasion. Fifteen years' research, however, into the history and antiquities of our race, may enable me to tell you *something* of our past history, both tradition and fact (for all history, both of nations and families, are about equally composed of both), and thus aid you in keeping posterity acquainted with the good deeds of our ancestors.

In the noble eulogy upon the great scholar, Swedenborg, delivered by Mr. Samuel Sandel, before the Royal Academy of Sweden, in the great Hall of the Nobles at Stockholm, occur these words:

"Nature and art form the ornaments of the earth; birth and education those of the human race. A fruit seed does not *always* produce a tree which yields as *excellent* fruit as that which produced *it;* which often is owing to the modifications effected on the tree by *art*, which occasion a difference in its *products*, but do not at all alter its nature. Experience supplies us with a great many *similar* instances in our own species. But it would be hazarding a paradox were we to attempt to determine *how far* certain virtues are *hereditary* in families, or are *introduced* into them by education. Be this as it may, it cannot be denied that having sprung from a virtuous and respectable family, inspires a man with confidence, when he is conscious that he does not disgrace his descent. In *every* condition (of life) it is a real advantage to be born in a family which has been, for a long time, the abode of honor and virtue, and a nursery of citizens every way useful to their country."

In addition to these words of Mr. Sandel, I would say that there is no peculiar merit to be attached to a family that have, for ages, maintained their proud and lofty positions by the *mere* possession of *great* estates, and certain special privileges, entailed for generations, and hereditary titles secured to them by the laws of the land, and which *makes* them counsellors of the realm, and the arbiters of the destinies of millions of their fellow men, by the *mere* right of birth, whether *nature* has *filled* them for such or not. But when a family, living in a republic like ours, where competition for the highest State and National offices, is open to all who have the requisite ability and energy to *reach* them, and *when* reached, to *fill* them, can maintain, unbroken, for over two centuries their prestige as soldiers, statesmen, jurists, scholars, and divines, and fill the highest offices in the State and National Governments, whether legislative, executive, judicial, ministerial or military, with credit and ability, and whose reputation and honor have never suffered a stain. they certainly deserve the reverence and esteem of their fellow citizens, and it is but just to them, that a record of their lives and their works should be preserved to posterity.

I think I may safely assert, my friends and kinsmen, that to *such* a race do *we* belong. Although no high-sounding title has ever been coupled with our name, and marked us as hereditary counsellors of England's monarchs, yet from the time of the Norman Conquest, we have lived upon our own estates, administering as county magistrates, justice in a limited circle, defrauding none, and recognized by that much abused, yet grandest of all human appellations—gentlemen.

Always maintaining the cause of truth, honesty and liberty of conscience, suffering *much* for conscience's *sake*, our race have never swerved from the path of right and duty. When persecution and tyranny raged in our beloved mother-land, the stern Puritans, Nathaniel Dickinson and Philemon Dickinson, and the gentle Quaker, Walter Dickinson, left the shores of Old England, to seek in the wilderness of America, a spot where they could, without fear of molestation, worship God according to the dictates of their conscience. Reared in the traditions of a race, who for six centuries had braved tyranny in every form, from the Norman **Rufus to the** unfortunate Charles Stuart, is it to be marveled at, that persecuted at home, the same spirit that impelled their warlike sires to fight manfully with the Barons against the tyrant, John, which ended in the glories of Runnymede, and to follow Cœur de Leon and Prince Edward to Palestine, led these three brave men, whose names I have just mentioned, to seek in the wilds of America, "freedom to worship God!"

Genealogy is a subject which we Americans, in our haste to get rich, have sadly neglected. It has too often been looked upon as a means to foster self-love and false pride; but that is the *abuse*, not the *true use* of this noble science, and I am glad to see, of late years, a growing taste among the descendants of our old Colonial and Revolutionary families, to learn more of the family history of the men who laid deep and strong, the foundations of our grand system of State and National Governments.

The names of Daniel S. Dickinson, of New York; Jonathan Dickinson, first President of Princeton College; Governors Mahlon and Philemon Dickerson, of New Jersey. Hons. Edward Dickinson, of Amherst; Rudolphus and Edward F. Dickinson, of Ohio; Isaac N. Dickerson, of New Jersey, all M. C's; and Wells S. Dickinson, State Senator, New York; and Andrew B. Dickinson, Minister to Nicaragua; all of the New England branches; and John Dickinson, L.L.D., Governor of Pennsylvania and Delaware, founder of Dickinson College, Carlisle, and the greatest political writer of his day; Gen. Philemon, of New York, afterwards United States Senator; Col. Henry Dickinson, Gen. Samuel Dickinson, first and second Judges; Walter, Samuel, James, Asa D., and Matthew C. Dickinson, Col. Henry Dickinson, Hons. James S., Henry S., David W., Amos, John, James, Jr., Hiram, John, Richard and William G. Dickinson, State Assemblymen, Presidential Electors and M. C's.; and Philemon Dickinson, for fifty years President of Trenton Banking Company, and a prominent state and county officer in New York, all of the Southern branch, should be written on the scroll of fame, and their memories cherished with tender feelings, by the race who bear the name these men have rendered so illustrious.

I am glad these family reunions are becoming more popular, year after year. The stronger the interest taken in them, the better for the government under which we live, and the less danger to be apprehended from Socialism, Communism and Anarchy. Every time we attend one, we go to our homes, better men, better women, better citizens, and better Christians.

In relation to our descent from the Plantagenets, through the marriage of Symon Dickinson and Catheryne Dudley, I am pleased to believe we inherited most of their *good* qualities, such as bravery, wisdom and courage.

I wish now to make a few remarks about the traditionary history of our race, and of the Southern branch of the Dickinson family. The facts relative to Ivar and Rollo, are taken from the history of Scandinavia, published by Professor Philip H. Dunham, of the University of Oxford, and from Burke's Extinct Peerage, article "Sinclair." Nearly eleven centuries ago, there appeared at the Court of Halfdan Huilbein, King of Norway, a soldier of fortune, named Ivar, a native of the Uplands, in Norway. He was said to have been, originally, a shepherd, and to have followed his flocks and herds on the craggy and ice-bound sides of the Saehattan, a snow-capped peak of the Uplands, towering eight thousand feet above the sea; but one day he was captured by a roving band of Northmen, and carried off to sea, to lead the life of a rover, and after a series of adventures by land and sea, during which period he is said to have visited the coasts of New Foundland and New England; he made his appearance at the Norse King's Court, about the year 700.

Being of handsome presence, and stalwart build, he soon became a great favorite with the King, who advanced him from one post to another, until he became General of his army, and was created Prince of the Uplands. But a still greater honor awaited this illustrious child of fortune. In 720, Halfdan bestowed upon him, in marriage, the hand of his only child, and the heiress of the realm —his daughter Eurittea. Halfdan died in 725, leaving his crown to his grandson, Eystein, a child of four summers. Ivar was regent during his son's minority. Eystein reigned until 755, leaving a successor, Harold Harfagn, and another son, Rogenwald, Earl of Maere, and Raumdahl, in Norway, who obtained from his brother Harold, a grant of the Shetland and Orkney Isles. Among other issues, Rogenwald left Rolfor Rollo, the most adventurous Prince of his age, who overran Normandy in 910. His sixth and youngest son, Walter, received the town and Castle of Caen, as his inheritance. His great grandson, Gaultier de Caen (Walter of Caen), accompanied William the Conqueror to England. From him sprang John de Caen, clerk in Chancery, reign of Edward I., and from him is supposed to have sprung Hugh Dicconsin, reputed grandfather of John of Leeds.

Let us now pass on to the third son of Symon Dickinson and Catheryne Dudley. Charles of London was born at Bradley, about the year 1590, and after receiving a liberal education, settled in London, where in the course of time he became an eminent merchant. He died in 1653, leaving by Rachael Carter, three sons—first, Walter; second, Henry; third, John. These three brothers became converts to the peculiar teachings of George Fox. In 1654, all three came to the Province of Virginia, arriving at Williamsburg in the spring or early summer of that year.

Walter, the eldest of the three, was born late in 1620, or in January, 1621, for he was baptized at St. Andrews,

Holborne, London, February 10, 1621. He seems to have followed his father's business, that of a merchant, and to have early engaged in the service of the London Company, as an emigration commissioner or agent. He received a grant of fifty acres of land for every adult person he sent to Virginia. The first patent for land bears date, September 6, 1654, and was for eight hundred acres of land near Merry Point, on the Rappahannock, in Lancaster County. He settled on this tract, and married the daughter of his neighbor, Jane Yarrett. In the early Winter of 1658–'59, he was obliged to flee from Virginia, on account of the religious persecutions against the Quakers. He located for a time at North Point, on the Potapsco river, near Baltimore, and in the Autumn of 1659, removed to Talbot County, Maryland. Here, in 1660, he bought a plantation, which he named "Croisedore," meaning "Golden Crusader," in memory of his ancestors, who followed the Banner of the Cross to Palestine. This plantation has descended in the direct male line to the present head of the house, Samuel T. Dickinson, of New York, and is occupied by that gentleman's brother, Mr. Overton Dickinson. Walter, in 1679, was commissioned one of the Judges of the Talbot County Court, serving until his death, in March, 1681. This was the first office held by *our* line in America. By his first wife, he left two sons—William and Charles, the latter of whom died young. His second wife was Mary Means. By her he had two children—Walter and Rachael. Walter's line is now extinct. William Dickinson, the eldest son of Walter, was born on the Rappahannock, in December, 1658. He was a merchant. He never held any political office. He married Elizabeth Powell, and dying in 1717, left three children—first, Elizabeth; second, Samuel; third, James. Elizabeth Dickinson was the wife of William Harrison. Their daughter, Rachael Harrison, married John Leeds, Surveyor General of Maryland, Clerk of Talbot County Court, Treasurer of the Eastern Shore, Maryland, and Judge of Talbot County Courts. Their daughter Rachael, married a Mr. Bozman. This gentleman's son, John Leeds Bozman, was the distinguished historian of Maryland, and his sister Rachael, married a gentleman named Kerr, and was the mother of John Leeds Kerr, M. C. from Maryland, United States Senator, Presidential Elector in 1841, and a member of the Harrisburg Convention, which nominated Harrison for the Presidency. His son, John Bozman Kerr, was a member of the Maryland Legislature, Deputy Attorney General, Charge d'Affairs to Nicaragua, Deputy Attorney General United States, and Solicitor of the Court of Claims. James Dickinson, was High Sheriff of Talbot County, Judge of the County Court, and member of Assembly. I have in my possession an original transcript from his docket, dated September 9, 1768, which was found among the Chew papers, at Germantown. His daughter married Rev. Thomas Bacon, D.D., a famous divine of his day. Samuel Dickinson, the eldest son of William, was born in 1690, educated at Oxford, and read law and practiced extensively in the Courts of Maryland, Delaware and Pennsylvania. In 1740, he became President Judge of the newly organized Court of Common Pleas, in Kent County, Delaware, and in 1754, Associate Judge of the Supreme Court of Delaware. He died in 1760. By his first wife, Judith Troth, he had, with eight others, a son Henry, who inherited "Croise-dore." This gentleman was Treasurer of the Eastern Shore of Maryland, many years, and a delegate to the Maryland Constitutional Convention of 1776. His more distinguished descendants, are, first—Samuel Dickinson, Inspector-General of Grain, Eastern Shore of Maryland; second—Philemon, M.D., Member of Assembly; third—Henry, Colonel of Militia, and Clerk of Dorchester County Courts; fourth—Solomon, Member of

Assembly, Judge of Orphans' Court, Brigadier-General of Militia; fifth—Samuel S., Judge of Levy Court, and Commissioner of Lotteries; sixth—Peter S., United States Marshal and Postmaster at Trappe, killed by a fall from his horse, at Easton, March 8, 1824.

Samuel Dickinson, by his second wife, Mary Cadwalader, had, first—John, of whom hereafter; second—Thomas; third—Philemon, Major-General of New Jersey Militia, Member of Provincial Congress, Member of Continental Congress, Vice-President of State Council, and United States Senator. *His* grandsons were, first—Philemon, Member of New Jersey Constitutional Convention, 1873, President of the Board of Commissioners of the State Sinking Fund, and President of the Trenton Banking Company nearly fifty years; second—my father, Samuel, Captain of the Tenth United States Infantry in the Mexican War, and Colonel of the First New Jersey Militia. This finishes Walter's descendants.

Of Henry, the second of the three emigrant brothers, we know nothing further than that he settled either in Louisa or Caroline County. His more distinguished descendants have been, Major Dickinson, who fell at Monmouth; General Samuel Dickinson, of Kentucky; Hon. David W. Dickinson, M. C., from Pennsylvania; Hon. James S. Dickinson, of Alabama, and Henry Dickinson, of Mississippi, President Electors; Hon. Asa D. Dickinson, member of Virginia Assembly and Senate and Judge of Common Pleas; Hiram Dickinson, Amos Dickinson and Matthew Dickinson, all Members of Assembly, and the latter a Judge of Common Pleas; and S. W. Dickinson, M.D., a distinguished physician of his native state and a medical writer of note.

Of John, the third of the three emigrant brothers, we know that his *eldest* son John settled in Talbot, and some of *his* descendants are in Delaware. His *youngest* son, William, settled in Plymouth, Montgomery County,

Pennsylvania. Hon. Mahlon H. Dickinson, late Chief Commissioner of Highways, and President of the State Board of Charities, and Dr. Hiram Corson, belong to this line.

Time forbids me to trespass longer on your patience. Our name is to be found in all the *higher* walks of life. We have produced men eminent in the law, in the halls of Congress, on the tented field, in the hospital, in the colleges, and in the pulpit; and many more in the ranks of commerce and finance. I think I may venture to say that all have been a credit and honor to the race from which they sprung, and that the family escutcheon, that has been handed down to us from the days of the Plantagenets, and which was a shining mark for the arrows of Mussulmen before the walls of Jerusalem, has suffered no stain or dishonor from our hands during the six centuries it has been our insignia.

Before I close, a word of tribute to the *noblest* Roman of them all—John Dickinson, L.L.D., Governor of Delaware and Pennsylvania, member of the Stamp Act Congress, Continental Congress, and *Federal* Constitutional Convention, and that of Delaware; Speaker of the Delaware Assembly, and Vice-President of its Council; member of the Pennsylvania Assembly, Chief Justice of its high Court of Appeals, and Colonel of its First Battalion; Chairman of the Annapolis Convention, writer of the famous "Farmer's Letters," first and second "Petitions to the King," "Declaration to the Armies," "Address to the States," and to the "Inhabitants of Quebec," and first and second series of "Fabian Letters;" founder of Dickinson College, Carlisle, and the *only* member of the famous first Continental Congress that *adopted* the "Declaration of Independence," who went down into the ranks, shouldered his musket, and fought as a *private*, on the bloody fields of Brandywine and Germantown, and whose bravery and courage on those eventful days, won him the stars of a Brigadier ere the smoke of battle had yet rolled away.

They who can look back, in the annals of their race, on such a man, may *well* feel pride in that blood which worked in the principles, and flowed into the acts of the race whose unselfish integrity and gentle courtesy are best expressed in the simple and telling words of their family motto: "*Esse quam videre*" (To *be*, rather than to appear).

THE PRESIDENT—Reference has been made to-day to the fact that the Montague family held its re-union last year in Haverhill, and that that family and ours have been very closely united in the past. We are largely indebted for the success of this gathering to the untiring efforts of a gentleman resident of this town, not of our name, but of our blood, Mr. George Montague, whom I now ask to address you.

Mr. George Montague spoke as follows:

Mr. Chairman, Ladies and Gentlemen, Brothers and Sisters and Cousins of the Dickinsons—I greet you all with a friendly salutation. I am very thankful that I have lived to see the day when so many of the Dickinsons have assembled. You know that it is according to the order of our active modern times that the course of everything is onward; it is futureward. There are very few that go to the past in retrospection. The whole influence of life is toward the future, for some award, for some emolument to come from the future. But this great Dickinson assemblage is an exception to this rule. We have all come here as by one impulse, saying, "we will give one day to the thought of our ancestors," to the memory of those who have gone before us. We will think of their prayers, of the labors they underwent, when they had much less of the advantages we have, now—nay, none at all; and added to all that, they had battles to fight. They had an enemy ever at their doors and around them. They were continually in danger of being awakened at night by the savage whoop of the Indians; and no mother felt that her little ones were safe in those days.

What a contrast between that period and ours! If we can call to mind their sufferings, their trials, their toils, and contrast them with this easy-going life which we live, and this time when prosperity rests upon everything, when wealth is flowing into the country, when we are at peace with all the world, we shall gain something by this comparison.

I suppose that every man and woman in the world had two grandfathers each, respectively. I had two grandfathers, Richard Montague and Nathaniel Dickinson,— no, they were my ancestors; my grandfather was Richard Montague; the fifth in descent from Richard and Nathan Dickinson. But we are not to speak of the Montagues: we said enough about them twelve months ago. Now we are to say something about the Dickinsons. This Nathan Dickinson, who was my grandfather, was in his way, a great man. He had all the elements of greatness in his character, although he had very little intellectual culture. He had but one book, and that was the Bible, or else Baxter's Saint's Rest. But he read his Bible well; he was a godly man. He had four noble sons and he had four charming daughters, eight children in all; and the names of his sons were Nathan, Perez, Ezekiel and Samuel Fowler. How closely they adhered to the Scripture for their names in those times; and his daughters were Esther, Faithful, Irene, and Anna. And they were all noble specimens of gentlemen and ladies.

When this grandfather was twenty years of age, still a youth in years, a rapid express came with the intelligence that the French and Indians were coming down Lake Champlain and were going to attack the settlement that fall. It required but one week to get ready. Nathan went out to meet the French and Indians. He gave that year to the service of his country. Then he returned and raised his family of children. He went through the revolutionary war, and at its close he had prepared two sons for college. Having no education himself, he still knew the advantages and value of an education; and close as those times were, hard as everything was, no money worth anything but silver dollars, and a man having a hundred of them was considered rich. He had this little small amount of saving; he still carried two sons through college. One of them made his mark as a useful minister, Timothy Dickinson, whose name is on that chart (pointing to the family chart behind him), and one, Samuel Fowler Dickinson, mentioned also in this town as one of the founders of Amherst College. These two excellent men were born in a little house only one mile east of us. I had a photograph taken of it, as I was interested to see if the timbers were solid. It is lined with two-inch plank, set edge to edge, extending all round. The planks are solid and intact to this day, and there they stand now. That was a specimen of a man whose character has gone down to the present time.

I don't know how many ministers there were in that family; I know there were four lawyers and many farmers and many active business men all over this country, eminated from that family, raised and reared in that house, and have gone out doing good. That is one instance of what the Dickinsons have done, one family.

Now I don't suppose that taking away of one stone from an elegant structure would occasion that structure to fall down. It would still stand, but there would be a defect; to remove a single stone from a splendid structure is to leave a defect in the structure. I don't say that taking away of a single Dickinson from the whole family would occasion its destruction; but I say that the Dickinsons have added their quota to all of the interests in this world, which have made themselves known. Whatever has made this structure—commercial, educational, mechanical, all the industries which have made us a great people, made us honored among the most eminent nations of the earth, still increasing in greatness—I say the Dickinsons have added their part, and have done it well.

I don't wish to detain you longer by my remarks. It was very far from my thoughts to say anything; having given my exertions to bringing you together, I am happy to look in your faces. I have all of the honor that I require, and I ask for nothing more. Therefore I will leave the stand.

THE PRESIDENT—I ought to say right here that tomorrow we are to have an excursion to Hadley and Mt. Holyoke. I have not had time to consult the committee in regard to the matter, but I suppose that ten o'clock will be the hour that we shall be expected to leave. About ten o'clock. The ladies and gentlemen will use the room in front. There will be a business meeting in the morning. I hope that everybody present will find time to be here. As it is very important that we should form an association and perpetuate these pleasant associations and recollections, and that is the hour to be devoted to that purpose.

The Chairman of the Finance Committee informs me that there is still a deficiency of two hundred dollars or more, and that the friends will be expected to contribute again if they all have contributed. This situation reminds me of a little story, which was told me by one of my class-mates here in Amherst, who went out to teach the Freedmen. He succeeded in establishing a church, and dedicating it. But they were unable to pay for it; and it was thought to be disgraceful to have that debt, and they gave up one entire day to it. They had a meeting in the afternoon and took up a collection, and another in the evening and took up a collection; and in the evening they brought out their most distinguished speaker, a quaint old colored gentleman. "Bruddren," said he, "I 'spose you tink we call upon you pretty often, but, you know, when you want to have a good cow, you must milk her dry every time."

I suppose the Finance Committee appeal to us on that ground.

This family takes great satisfaction in the development of the educational interests of this commonwealth. Those under the direction of the authority of the commonwealth are in the charge of one of our own name, and I now have the pleasure of presenting to you John W. Dickinson, of our family, of Boston, Secretary of the State Board of Education.

Mr. Dickinson delivered the following address:

My Brothers and Sisters of the Dickinson Family— It is well known to some of you, that, after a long absence, I am just coming back into an active life. My misfortune has prevented me from rendering any assistance to the officers chosen to organize this gathering of the living members of our race, and it will continue to prevent me from taking any important part in the exercises of the meeting itself. Although I may not contribute anything to the enjoyment of others who are present at this gathering, I shall contribute much to my own pleasure, in simply being here, and in looking into the faces of those who claim to be twigs from the same branch of the great human tree.

We are many in number, but we are made one in spirit, by having descended from the same original stock, and by inheriting those common qualities which distinguish us from all other people, and which will, through all coming time, bind us together in one distinct family.

I have heard it said by members of our family, who have made careful observations, that the Dickinsons, wherever in the world they may be found, bear to one another, both a physical and mental resemblance. The principle of evolution that is slowly working its changes in all living things, may have added some new elements to the individual members of the present race; but, still, I do not doubt that every one of them has, to a marked degree, some of the characteristics which made old Nathaniel a distinct and independent member of the early Wethersfield Church.

The physical body of a genuine Dickinson, taken at its maturity, is somewhat above the ordinary height, but not generally burdened with a superabundance of useless flesh. It is straight and compact in its structure. Some of the features of the face are inclined to be prominent, presenting the sure external marks, according to the judgments of Julius Cæsar and the elder Napoleon, of the existence of that intellectual constitution which makes sharp thinkers and brave soldiers. The members of the race having generally inherited good physical structures, and the power of self-control, live to a good old age.

In their mental constitutions, the members of the family show, also, that they have a common origin. I have never known one of them to confess that he was mistaken until he was fully convinced of his error; and I have never known or heard of many convictions. I do not mean to say that they are inclined to close their eyes against the truth, but I rather suppose that before their judgments are formed, they are accustomed to think so long and accurately, that the truth is quite surely found. This firmness of which I speak is especially exhibited in matters of faith, pertaining to politics and religion, and yet I have known it to show itself in the common affairs of life. If it is controlled by that higher principle of human action, a sense of duty; it is one of the most important elements of a strong and consistent character. It will not allow the individual possessing it to forsake a principle, though urged by policy or convenience, or by any consideration which appeals simply to the selfish principle of action. This element of character, as it sometimes exhibits itself, is well illustrated by an event which happened many years ago in a neighboring town.

The church and society of the town were considering the propriety of keeping as holy time, Sunday rather than Saturday evening, Saturday evening having been before that, from the most ancient times, observed as a part of the Sabbath day. The reasons given for the change were, that the merchants of the place could not conveniently close their stores at sunset on Saturday night ; nor could the farmers and their households always close the labors of the week promptly at that time. After some discussion of the subject, the churches and their societies concluded to take a vote on the subject. Papers were distributed on which the will of the people was to be expressed. When the votes were collected it was found that a good Deacon of the parish, whose faith was not to be affected by mere human convenience, had written on his paper the following expression of his will, with reference to the proposed change: "Not strenuous. Always have kept Saturday night, and always shall."

Such an element of character, if set free from prejudice by a liberal culture, makes reliable and successful men. It probably brought our ancestor from Wethersfield to Hadley, and enabled him to endure with heroic fortitude the pain caused by the separation from old friends and old associations, and to become one of the leading spirits in the new settlement. The members of the family have not, in modern times, been noted for their inclination or success in amassing large stores of physical wealth, and yet they have all been thrifty people, always possessing enough; but, like true philosophers, they have believed that money is good for nothing except for what it will buy. They have generally acted on the principle that it is a wise thing to convert as much material wealth as possible into something that can be added to the individual as an everlasting possession; and so they have freely exchanged it for that which will cultivate the intellect, and gratify the taste, and satisfy the conscience. I have heard it said, however, that in more ancient times there was a Dickinson who succeeded in adding to his mental and moral wealth large stores of physical riches, and that these riches ought, by the natural laws of inheritance, to be distributed among his descendants. For one, as much as I despise physical wealth, considered apart from its relations to higher and better things, I should be exceedingly pleased to have this distribution made, even in my own day.

Another characteristic of the race is found in its love of the humorous. Humor is a quality of mind, and has for its object those innocent weaknesses and foibles which we do not really care to possess ourselves, but which we are often pleased to find possessed by others. This quality of mind frequently leads one to the performance of those acts which excite emotions of the ludicrous, and which are illustrated by anecdotes and sayings invented by somebody, and repeated by others for the amusement of the company.

I have known persons closely related to me by blood, full of those anecdotes, that describe the mental peculiarities of which I have spoken. These stories are often repeated on proper occasions, and they never lose either their interest or their pith by the repetition; for an active imagination is sure to clothe them with new beauty as often as they chance to reappear.

The family is noted also for its love of kindred. This love is expressed by the friendly social intercourse that not only the members of the same household constantly maintain with one another, but that each individual ever maintains with all others of his kind. The intercourse, I know by experience, is not unfrequently marked by that unselfishness which one is conscious of possessing when he prefers another to himself. The individuals of the race have an inherited pride of birth, which has come along down through the generations, and which gives evidence of a consciousness of an honorable origin of good blood flowing in the veins.

Dickinson is a good name in the country. Many good and noted men have been called by it. Theologians and lawyers and statesmen of this name have won an honorable place in human history, by their good deeds and their heroic lives; while a multitude of others have adorned their private lives by the practice of all the virtues.

We, their descendants, shall do well if we maintain in our lives, and in our intercourse with one another and with the world, the noble character of our fathers.

I suppose it is proper, on an occasion like this, for each one of us to say a word concerning his own place in the Dickinson family.

My father's name was William Dickinson. He was born in old Hadley, in the year 1785, and in the house now standing at the foot of Middle street. The house was built by my grandfather. It stands on a beautiful spot, commanding a good view of the Connecticut, of that most charming of all New England villages, Northampton, of the famous Northampton and Hadley Meadows, and of grand old Mount Holyoke, the back bone of the Connecticut Valley.

The house, I am glad to say, has always been occupied by the descendants of him who laid its ancient foundation. It is now inhabited by a genuine Dickinson, possessing, to a marked degree, all the physical and mental peculiarities that make him a good type of the race to which he belongs. I only wish he too had a son, who, inheriting the sterling good qualities of his father, could continue, in unbroken succession, the Dickinson possession of the sacred old home of my ancestors.

As I have already said, my father was born in 1785. He was the son of John Dickinson, who was the son of John, who was the son of William, who was the son of Nehimiah, who was the son of the historic Nathaniel.

So that my brothers and sisters were but six generations away from him whom we call our common ancestor.

My father was an intense member of our race. He left Hadley while he was yet a young man, but he never forgot the home of his youth, nor his kindred and friends. Throughout his life his thoughts were ever busy with the scenes of his childhood. All his anecdotes and familiar illustrations of the affairs of common life bore some relation to the events of his early life, and he was over-joyed whenever he could return again to the place of his birth. For forty years he held the office of Deacon of a Congregational church, and during his long life of Christian service he never intentionally performed an act in public or in private that would bring dishonor to the sacred cause for whose success he ever labored and prayed, and when he died, the whole community, as one man, were ready to honor his memory. His family of nine children, with but one exception, reached mature life before they were called to separate from one another by that separation that knows no earthly reunion.

One only besides myself of the number is able to be present and participate in this glad reunion. That one is a brother, whom I have every reason to honor and to love. My friends, I trust this meeting of our family will be the occasion of increasing our love for one another, and our high regard for the memory of our noble ancestors.

LETTER FROM DON M. DICKINSON.

The President—Reference to the programme will show you that the toastmaster was to be Don M. Dickinson, of Michigan. No one can regret his absence more than I do; he is a gentleman of the most brilliant qualities, and one of the foremost members of the Bar in Michigan. I have a letter in which he pleads business engagements which he cannot escape, as the reason why he is not here to-day:

"Detroit, Mich.,
"Aug. 6th, 1883.

"M. F. Dickinson, Jr., Esq., care Mr. F. W. Dickinson, Amherst, Mass.:

"My Dear Sir—I have your very kind letter of second instant. I have been much interested in the proposed reunion of the family, and had fully intended to be present, with my father. If there were anything which would add to my regret over the disappointment at my inability to be present, it would be the failure to meet you, and the loss of the pleasure it would be to aid in bearing up your hands. I am in the midst of a railroad fight which will last a week yet, and anticipate the necessity of going to England immediately after the conclusion of the trial. I had expected that the suit would terminate before the reunion, and that I might snatch the time to be with you, before any other engagement would occupy me, but the trial itself will detain me. I trust that there may be a full delegation from the Virginia branch, and that the Massachusetts and Southern stock may dwell together, in old Amherst, in unity. You will observe by the list of toasts suggested by me, that their presence was anticipated.

"I suggest, as in the second proposed toast, that to the present time our good name has never been sullied by any bearer of it, high or low, rich or poor.

"With most heartfelt regrets that I cannot join you,

and with the best wishes for a happy and successful meeting. I am, my dear friends,

"Very Truly Yours,
"Don M. Dickinson.

"P. S.—I am a delegate, I believe, to the National Bar Association, meeting at Saratoga on the twenty-third instant, and if, in the country, shall attend, and then hope to meet you.   "D."

The President—A telegram has been received by the Secretary, from Colorado Springs, a distant point in our country, which I will read.

"Colorado Springs, Col.,
August 7, 1883.

"F. W. Dickinson:

"Cordial greetings from descendants of the late Nathan Dickinson, native of Amherst. We join with the assembled family to-day in veneration of our ancestral names.

"Mrs. D. L. Gillette,
"Mary A. Dickinson, and
"Elizabeth B. Dickinson."

The President—It is a very interesting fact, that wherever we may go in the country, it is impossible to travel five hundred miles without meeting some stranger bearing the same name, or some person descended from our common stock. I was, three or four years ago, in Salt Lake City; I went under the guidance of a young Englishman who was living at Salt Lake City. While there I met a number of prominent men of the city, and among them was one to whom I was introduced; he said, "this is Mr. Dickinson, of Boston." It was General D, H. Wells. The General rendered very distinguished service to the country in driving out the Indians; these services were recognized and rewarded by the government. He said, after being introduced, "Dickinson, Dickinson,—my mother was Experience Dickinson." "Yes," said I, "probably from Weathersfield, Connecticut." "Yes, that is so; her father's name was Elijah Dickinson." I have traced the matter up since then and find that he was descended from Nathaniel Dickinson. He sent his son to call on me—a gentleman who is very much interested in genealogical subjects. We had a very interesting talk, and it was a very pleasant acquaintance.

I sent an invitation to General Wells to attend this meeting. I have received a very interesting letter from him, and I am going to take the liberty of reading it to you. I suspect that two of his daughters are in the audience. At any rate, he commends to our attention two ladies, who are temporary residents of this place:

"SALT LAKE CITY,
"July 28, 1883.

"*M. F. Dickinson, Jr.:*

"DEAR SIR—I sincerely thank you for your very welcome letter, dated July 23d, which was received yesterday with much pleasure. I fully appreciate the kind feelings expressed, and am very grateful for the cordial invitation extended to me and also to my son, to attend the Dickinson meeting, at Amherst, Mass., on the eighth and ninth of August, proximo.

"Some little time ago I received copy of circular, giving information concerning this reunion, and thought then, as I do now, that I was indebted to you for the courtesy, and have been intending to write ever since—indeed, I had a letter already commenced when your favor of the twenty-third was received.

"I remember distinctly the introduction you allude to, and the brief interview with you at the time. Also, the conversation about the Dickinsons. I regret exceedingly my inability to attend the meeting, as I feel assured it will be an interesting event, and I am greatly interested in the subject of genealogy. If I could in any way contribute to the interest of the occasion, I should be most happy to do so, but my knowledge of the ancestry of the Dickinsons is very limited. I will, however, state what I do know briefly. My father was Daniel Wells, son of Joshua Wells, my grandfather, and of Experience Dickinson Wells, of Weathersfield, Connecticut. Experience Dickinson, my grandmother, was the daughter of Elihu Dickinson ; this was about the extent of my information, previous to receiving your letter, which gives me a few more items concerning my progenitors, the Dickinsons, and for which I am deeply indebted. I am greatly interested in the family, and shall look forward with pleasure to the benefits resulting from the meeting, and shall hope to receive, through your courtesy and generosity, particulars of the proceedings, and information which will lead to an enlarged acquaintance with my relatives, and knowledge of my ancestors of the Dickinson lineage.

"I hope that a full and complete genealogical account will be obtained and published, giving details, dates and names, when and where born, and dates of deaths, from the earliest settlement in America ; and, also, connecting with the family in the old country, tracing back as far as possible, including branches of both male and female line, and as many of the collateral branches as can be obtained.

"Such a book I should esteem of great value, and would contribute the names of all the descendants of Experience Dickinson that I could obtain. My son, whom you so kindly invited, is absent at present from home, on a trip to the Yellowstone river, or he would certainly have replied by letter to your cordial invitation, but will, I am sure, take pleasure in writing to you after his return.

LETTER FROM DANIEL H. WELLS.

"I feel justly proud of my relationship to the Dickinson family, and send congratulations to all my kindred assembled to celebrate the two hundred and twenty-third anniversary of the settlement of Nathaniel Dickinson in Hadley, Massachusetts. May a spirit of peace and love pervade the meeting, and abide with you in all your deliberations and associations together, and the most perfect success attend your endeavors to gather and to disseminate a knowledge of the family history, and that a book may be compiled and published ready for circulation at an early date, that those now living may reap the reward of the labor.

"I trust it may be my good fortune to meet some of my kindred of this branch of my pergenitors, and become better acquainted with facts in relation to their history. Tourists are constantly visiting Salt Lake City, and it is but natural to suppose that some of the Dickinsons may find their way out here on business or pleasure.

"Again thanking you for courtesy, etc., and hoping and believing that you will have an enjoyable season at the family gathering, I am, very respectfully,

"Yours fraternally,

"DANIEL H. WELLS."

"P. S.—I take the liberty of referring my two daughters, who are now visiting relatives in Thorndike, near Palmer, and who will probably attend the meeting of the Dickinson family at Amherst, to you for favorable reception and attention."

THE PRESIDENT—In the list of toasts prepared by Mr. Don M. Dickinson, is this one: "Our family, God bless us, every one."

I ask Judge William F. Dickinson, of Aurora, Ill., to respond to this sentiment.

Judge Dickinson spoke as follows:

Mr. President and fellow kinsmen Just why the honor of responding to so noble a sentiment was referred to me, I am unable to understand, except from the total ignorance of the committee as to myself. They may have judged me to be a man of words, capable to do a subject of that kind justice, while the fact is far otherwise. I cannot better illustrate my feelings in being called upon to respond to the sentiment at the present time, after what has been said in your presence, than to relate a story personal to myself. It was my fortune, some forty years since, to be traveling on a Mississippi river steamboat, in company with a personal friend. At a point on the river, just after we passed Vicksburg, a party of civil engineers came on board, headed by a tall, burly, well-looking gentleman. The weather being cold, the party soon gathered about the stove in the cabin, where I was conversing with my friend. From his standing near me he heard my friend call me by name at that moment. Whereupon he looked down upon me and said: "Is your name Dickinson?" To which I politely assented: "It is." He then surveyed my person from head to foot, with the remark, "well you must have sprung from a mighty sight smaller origin than I did." As I ventured to seek his acquaintance, he soon traced his origin to old Amherst, Massachusetts, which to me well accounted for his modesty.

What shall I say of our family? Nothing whatever. After listening to the letters and addresses we have listened to this morning, giving a pretty full and extended history of our family, it is eloquent in me to keep absolutely silent. I feel that it would take an immensely large volume to contain all that I *don't* know about the family; while a sheet of foolscap would contain all that I do know. Therefore I shall not attempt even an allusion to our family. But in response to the sentiment, "God bless us, every one," I will say that no grander sentiment was ever uttered than Dickens puts into the mouth of Tiny Tim, when he says, "God bless us, every one." It cannot be enlarged upon; it means far more than God bless you, or God bless me; it covers all. I leave it where it was left by Tiny Tim. We have now partaken of the goose and pudding, not furnished by Mrs. Cracket, which so inspired Tiny Tim, and may it prove equally inspiring, when we have accomplished all the objects for which we came together, that we may separate with new kindred ties, more extended ideas and advanced feelings, and when we put up our petition, it shall not be our prayer, "God bless me and my wife, my son John and his wife, us four, no more," but that broader, nobler sentiment, "God bless us, every one." We shall be better men, better women, and better citizens, when that is accomplished.

THE PRESIDENT—I call upon Mr. William L. Dickinson, Superintendent of Schools, of Jersey City, New Jersey, to address you.

Mr. W. L. Dickinson spoke as follows:

I have enjoyed this meeting very much, and I think the committee who has got this thing up and provided this entertainment are worthy of all praise. I have no fault to find, but great praise for all that they have done except one: when they called upon me without preparation at the commencement of these exercises, to reply to this sentiment, embodying so much, I think they made a mistake, and I hope they will not repeat any such mistake.

But here we are to-day, we Dickinsons, and I am glad, as one of our speakers has said, to see so many whose name I know, if I don't know their faces. I thought the Dickinsons were a large and important family, looking at home; and I have been satisfied with what I found there.

But I didn't think that we drew our blood from the veins of the old Scandinavians who overthrew the Roman Empire; I didn't think we belonged to the Duke of Normandy, who conquered England's sometime king. I felt like raising my head a little higher. I live near New York, and there I have been accustomed to meet a great many persons with a great many names; and I was surprised to find an Irishman, who was a Dickinson, who talked with a bit of a brogue, and who was very fond of "poteen;" I suppose that some of us once lived in Ireland; and I did come across a genuine perfectly coal black negro, who had the name of William Dickinson. I think our reverend brother might have gone back a little further; and if he had traced the family back to Ham, I should not have been surprised. I have no doubt that he can trace us back to Noah at any rate.

These allusions to the glory of the Dickinson family have made my blood thrill; I have felt my heart beat faster; I have felt bigger than I ever felt before. When he has told of the wonderful achievements which they have wrought, extending back to the time of Charles of England. There was a certain famous Dr. Edmund Dickinson, whose life I had the pleasure of reading not long ago. Wherever the Dickinsons have appeared in any branch of business, science, art, labor, they have always conducted themselves well. They have not been as brilliant as Napoleon Bonaparte, but they have always stood on high ground, and shown themselves good solid foundation for a man to rest upon. And I have thought over this matter, and what is the secret of all this? How is it that they have stood so high? How is it they stand such a survival of the fittest, through so many generations? We find them standing on a high level, and we find that they have been looked up to as good citizens, and have received the respect and advancement of such offices as could be bestowed by their fellow men. I think it is worth while to ask the reason for all this. Men don't rise to great eminence through devotion to vice; that is, not for a great length of time; they don't rise through any selfish purposes. An individual man may for a time raise himself above others by devotion to some particular vice or some particular immorality. He may raise himself above his fellow men for a time, but that is sure to run out. No family ever lived two hundred years at that rate. Now, what was the reason of it all? What is the riddle? I think I have found it. We recollect that our fathers built themselves on the Lord God. Out of that blessed book they learned this virtue, that patience, that strength, which has made them conspicuous before the world. I think that there you will find the secret of it all. I think if we are to transmit to our descendants those virtues which our ancestors have shown, if we are to continue through a hundred years to come, and to show a family, broad, square, and honest, upon which the fate of an empire may rest, it will be because we still cling to those same virtues, still honor that same book which our ancestors, and which I believe those living now, do honor.

Time waxes. It is not necessary for me to dilate upon this subject. I came without preparation; I think I cannot close without exhorting all those who are present to learn to honor these ancestors of ours, and to seek the sources of their strength, and to build themselves up on the same models upon which they built.

THE PRESIDENT.—The last speaker is an illustration of how well a Dickinson can do who does not prepare himself. I shall ask Mr. George H. Corson, of Morristown, Pennsylvania, to address the audience.

Mr. Corson spoke as follows:

Ladies and Gentlemen:—From the time that the visions presented themselves to John at Patmos, down to the settlement of Petersburgh and Jamestown, there was not such a deliverance from error as in those two periods, from the time of the deliverance of Governor Berkely to the hanging of John Brown, and from the time of the revolution to the election of Abraham Lincoln. Two hundred years ago, Governor Berkely, of Virginia, could write to the Privy Council of England, and say, "Thank God! we have no free schools, and no printing, and I pray that we may not have this hundred years. For education brings disturbance, errors, and sects into the world, and printing divulges them and libels God's best government." Those were the days when women were sold as wives in Virginia, for one hundred pounds of tobacco, each valued at seventy-five dollars; when men were sent there for a period of one hundred years, banished from England; when tobacco was a legal tender currency, and when non-Conformists, Anabaptist and Quakers had notice to quit without ceremony.

Well, we will give Governor Berkely his hundred years, if you please, of absence of public schools and printing, and we will take the next hundred years, and especially the first score and the last score of this last century, for the measures which have made the Old Dominion conspicuous in the annals of the nations of the earth.

After this and after that period of which he spoke, came the era of the presidents, of the great rulers, and the greater than the presidents, the Patrick Henrys, the Henry Clays, the hosts of Dickinsons. But the old Bay State has always been proud of her presidents, as the old Dominion has. But I say to you now, look well to your laurels; henceforth perhaps all that you can claim in the White House will be its chief butler. The re-adjusters will give you legal tender for any party that seeks office for revenue only.

But I am not here to relate history or to make prophecies. All this has been done, and all this history has been well said to-day. I come here because I look upon this as the commencement of a great, social, loyal family union. For there is a deep meaning in social life. Restricted citizenship does not comprise the whole duty of man. A state cannot develope all the finer attributes of our nature, both by reason of its inability in a corporate capacity to appreciate their existence, and by reason of its inability to provide the necessary instrument for their exercise. It may nourish patriotism, and it may probably warm the blood of the heart in love of home, and in defense of our native land. It may nourish large systems, promote those of clear brain, and develope the interests of the whole people. The government can do this ; strong muscles and strong minds and sinewy arms ; these things may direct in the good cause. But the man is higher than the citizen, and he can receive his proper development only in social life ; social intercourse, cordial sympathy, lasting friendship, make life roll off its troubles and its care. Social union can cultivate the soul, and by its magic influence, call into being ties of kindred, delicate as gossamer, but as lasting as life. Those old memories that spring up at the mention of home, bright dreams of sunnier hours, that send their trembling dew through all the currents of our future years. These feelings we should cherish, for surely there are trials and coldness and scorn enough in this life, and they will come soon enough to darken the hopes and crush the prospects of the young souls.

There is a deep meaning in all this literature ; that meaning is found in the wide experience of history, in the broad domain of philosphy, in the flowery fields of romance, on the starry pinacles of poetry. A man has felt these influences, as the Judge has well remarked a while ago, when he reads in romance of those principles which are the foundation of our morality and the support of religion. But there is a deep meaning in union, association—a marvelous power which is felt. Even the dew drops that gather upon the roses in the morning, may rend an oak or whirl an engine through the tunneled rock. Beyond this, it is the type of brotherhood; and man has felt its influence, when the demon of war has trampled queenly cities in the dust, and linked the energies of heroic hearts together, and the old republic has failed, that the new republic may spring from its ashes.

This glorious Union, whose boundaries are washed by two oceans, the genius of whose constitution is the spirit of human freedom, attests the blessing of political union; the world has its greatest blessing in the union of hearts, heads and hands. Union of hands to cultivate our soil, to tunnel our mountains, to bridge our cataracts; union of heads, to scale the heights of noblest thought, to penetrate the deep mysteries of science, to enter the glorious arena of art. The union of hearts binds up our broken hopes and teaches us to live nobly here that we may look forward to that reunion which awaits us beyond the grave.

There is deep meaning in the present time problem; king-craft with its wily diplomacy, and priest-craft with its hoary superstition, are yielding already to the advance of the principles of freedom. Nature assists mankind to enlarge the understanding and intellect. Science goes down toward the earth's central fires to read the history of our creation; it goes up toward Heaven to fetter the thunderbolt for human use. There is a deep meaning in social life; there is a deep meaning in literature; a deep meaning in union; and from these three interests, by these means comes this social family union of to-day.

LETTER FROM A. D. DICKINSON.

THE PRESIDENT—It is proper at this time that I should read briefly from two or three letters received from gentlemen in the South, who are of our common name and stock. The first one is from A. D. Dickinson, Springfield, Worsham Postoffice, Prince Edward County, Virginia, addressed to the secretary:

"SPRINGFIELD, WORSHAM POSTOFFICE,
PRINCE EDWARD COUNTY, VA.,
August 2d, 1882.

"*F. W. Dickinson, Secretary, 144 State Street, Springfield, Mass.:*

"MY DEAR SIR—Untoward circumstances, beyond my control, oblige me *most reluctantly* to forego the pleasure of meeting with you and other friends and kindred, at Amherst, on the eight and ninth of August, as I had hoped and intended. I cannot express the regret I feel at this disappointment.

"It would have given me infinite satisfaction, I am sure, to have participated in the family gathering. Be assured that my heart will be with you in sympathy and interest.

"Be pleased to make my respectful and kindly regards to our family friends, who, though personally unknown to me, are recognized as entitled to fraternal and even affectionate consideration.

"Unable to be present in person, I send herewith a photograph likeness, which I beg that you will do me the honor to accept.

"Very Truly, Your Friend and Relation,
"A. D. DICKINSON.

Another brief note, from William J. Dickenson (with an e), residing at North Bickley Mills:

"RIVERSIDE, NEAR BICKLEY MILLS,
RUSSELL COUNTY, VA.,
July 24, 1883.

"*Francke W. Dickinson, Secretary, &c.:*

"DEAR SIR—The program of the meeting of the Dickinson family at Amherst, August 8th, 1883, is received, for which thanks. I congratulate my New England cousins upon their enterprise. It is one worthy of the high character and standing of the family; an enterprise that should have been attended to many years ago, before the time of the settlement of the family in America became so beclouded and obscure, and before the descendants therefrom became so wide-spread and alienated. The Dickinson family, now in the United States, are almost equal in numbers to the Twelve Tribes of Israel. I hope the meeting may prove a success. That our ancestry may be traced up at this union of the family, so we may know our origin, which, doubtless, is a common one. I would be delighted to attend the union and participate in the festivities of that, to be, quite interesting occasion; but time and distance render it doubtful.

"Respectfully,
"WM. J. DICKENSON."

THE PRESIDENT—I hold two letters, from one of which I will read extracts, and I wish to say that it is from one of the most distinguished jurists of the South—Judge Alexander White, of Dallas, Texas. I have been connected with professional business, in which I have had frequent occasion to see him, and have enjoyed a very large correspondence with him, and have had letters enough to make a good sized volume. I found that he was descended from the Dickinsons; his mother was a Dickinson, from New Hampshire. He is a typical southern man, of most distinguished learning and acquirements, and has the reputation of being the ablest equity lawyer there. A man, who, before the war, owned a hundred slaves, who was in the highest position, both from his social position and his love of the South. He was member of Congress before the war.

I have been told that he was opposed to secession, but after his state, Alabama, went into secession, he went with it, and went into the army, shouldered his musket, refused to have a commission; and he remained in the army three years. I think most of the time in Alabama and neighboring states. The result of the war was disastrous to him, and destroyed all his property. After the war he was sent to Congress from the Selma District, as a Republican. He was on the Judiciary Committee with Governor Butler. He was appointed a Justice of Utah. He made a decision by which Brigham Young was discharged from arrest, upon a writ of *habeas corpus*. It threw some odium on Judge White, although I think the best lawyers think that he was right. But from the opposition, he withdrew his name from the Senate. He removed to Dallas, Texas, where he has since resided, and where he enjoys a very extensive and lucrative practice. I want to read to you a few extracts. I had anticipated great pleasure in having him here, and having you see him:

"TAMPASAS, Texas,
"August 2d, 1883.

"*M. F. Dickinson, Esq., Boston, Mass.:*

"DEAR SIR—The enclosed letter was written last night explaining why I could not attend the Dickinson meeting at Hadley, on the eighth. I had mistaken the date, but the difficulties of being there the eighth would be greater than to be there on the eighteenth. I cannot express to you the disappointment I experience in not being able to attend the meeting. I have long contemplated going at some leisure time to New Hampshire, and tracing up what I could of my mother's family; and now an occasion presents itself most favorable for such inquiries, and yet I cannot avail myself of the opportunity." *"My mother originated from Hadley, and I have often heard her speak of that place. My uncle, John Dickinson, graduated at Dartmouth College when very young He read law, and about 1808, came to Nashville, Tennessee, to practice his profession. He reached high distinction, and acquired what was then regarded, a large fortune, though he died young. He and Jenkins Whitesides were the recognized leaders of the Tennessee bar, and that among men, many of whom afterwards attained national reputation,— Grundy, Bell, Jackson, Benton, Carroll, and others. My mother came some years after my uncle, John Dickinson, to Nashville, accompanied by her brother, Dr. William G. Dickinson. My uncle, William, was well known in the medical world, as a physician and surgeon, and at the time of his death, in 1843, had long ranked as one of the ablest of his profession in the city. My father and mother married in Tennessee, and in the spring of 1822, moved to Alabama, where both lived the remainder of their lives. My father was Judge of the Circuit, and one of the Judges of the Supreme Court. My mother left three sons and two daughters. One of these last married a Mr. Dixon, a merchant of fine standing; she died many years since. The other daughter married Judge Joseph G. Baldwin, of the Supreme Court of California, and his son, Alexander W. Baldwin, was a Judge of the Federal Court, at twenty-seven years of age. He was killed by a railroad accident, and was regarded as the most promising young man of the Pacific Coast. Of the three sons, two are lawyers and one a physician.

*Extract from another letter.

"We had all attained success, and were respected where known. Pecuniarily, we had done well till the war. That toppled all at the South; and the higher before the crash, the farther the fall when it came.

"Since then, nothing notable except this,—that none of us yielded to despair, as thousands at the South did after the collapse. We all went to work, and have done our best to retrieve and rebuild. I regard this as the most distinctively Dickinson trait we have. We do not give in. We keep our flag flying, and propose to do so until we succumb to the inevitable, which overwhelms all.

"Unavoidably there is a vein of egotism and vanity in this. The subject and the occasion involve it. I have stated a few leading facts, with names of individuals of this branch of the Dickinson family, which so long ago wandered far away from the ancestral homestead, and from family and friends of the mother-land. I have been more free in praise than I would under the circumstances, that you may have the satisfaction of knowing that the family name here has been sustained in respectability and honor, among new and unfamiliar people in this distant southern land; not new to us, but once new to those from whom we are proved to have descended.

"With the hope that your reunion may afford much pleasure and happiness to all who are so fortunate as to be able to attend it, and warm wishes for your personal welfare, I am,

"Very Truly, Your Friend and Obedient Servant.

"ALEX' WHITE."

THE PRESIDENT—The next toast is, "The Mothers of Our Family." I will ask Mr. Stillman B. Pratt, of Marlboro, Massachusetts, to address us.

Mr. Pratt spoke as follows:

Friends of the Dickinson Family—I am a newspaper man, and I am independent of these speeches here, and can beg leave "to report in print." I will not detain this meeting further with any special remarks at this time. I can only say that I listened with the most thrilling interest of all, to the experience of that Dickinson mother, up there in that northern home, as she waits and waits for that son to be brought home,—the dead body on horse back, from that encounter with the Indians. I have laid that experience of that early mother, along with some experience in our own family, when we came to leave our Marlboro home for this family union. Our little boy was quite sick; we thought we had quite a family until he (the President) told us about the twenty-three children. Our little boy was quite sick; but we didn't have to wait for the slow prospect of a messenger on horse back to tell us how little Billy was getting on. We had only to turn to our telephone, and in a single moment we could hear little Billy, in his home at Marlboro, bid his mother good night, and kiss his hand. We could hear the sound of the kiss as it came to us. It seems to me that there is nothing to give a clearer picture of the grand advances that have been made, since the Dickinson family took possession of that square mile, than to lay alongside the experience of those two mothers. I hope that somewhere in this great family there will come a painter, or a poet laureate, who shall paint as Tennyson has the experience of that "Maiden of England," the poet or painter who shall put the picture of that Christian mother in those Indian times, upon canvass, because I believe it will be one of the most historic pictures of America.

THE PRESIDENT —I now call upon Henry B. Dickinson of Norristown, Pennsylvania, to address you.

This gentleman not being in the hall, the President called upon "one of the rising young farmers of the valley, whom I claim as a cousin, not merely by name but by blood, E. N. Dickinson of East street, as we call it, to respond."

Mr. Dickinson spoke as follows:

Mr. President, Ladies and Gentlemen—Whether applied to the entire farming realm or only to that portion whose veins are coursed by Dickinson blood, I heartily respond to the invitation. It is true that in the farming portion of our nation we join the bone, sinew, and strong common sense of the Republic. It is also equally true that great physical force and vitality acquired in country life, and the discipline received in the pursuit of rural affairs are the foundations of that intellectual power which enables its possessors to attain positions of eminence, usefulness and renown, and also to adorn the various professions and other walks of life, exhibitions of which we have heard here to-day. On this account and for this reason we find the farmers in the front rank at Quebec, at Lundy's Lane, at Cerro Gordo, at Bunker Hill, and last, but not least, the great war of the Rebellion, trailing in the dust the rags of secession and planting upon the battlements of the Rebellion the glorious old Stars and Stripes.

Agriculture is not only the foundation, but it is the impelling force of civilization. The advancing and receding wave of each harvest times the advance of the other industries. Our ancestor was a farmer; the very large proportion of his descendants are tillers of the soil; and it is on this account that they have been noted for their patriotism, for being lovers of liberty, and they have made advances in all the walks of life. It was this that gave them courage to defend their hearthstones from oppression and invaders; this has given them a character for stability, and that enduring interest in the common order and the advancement of the community in which they dwell, and led them to believe that the public weal was their own, and to put forth efforts for its highest good, and to remain constant in times of danger and adversity, as well as those of *safety* and prosperity. Mr. President, you may well be proud of the farmers that they stood and fired that wonderful shot that "echoed round the world," but something more than that ; this is true ; you should be faithful to them and remove every burden from their shoulders, for they laid the foundations on which the Republic was built, and they furnish the means of life and prosperity to all others.

THE PRESIDENT -Having called upon a cousin of mine, I feel now like calling upon a brother ; he has done me a great many injuries, and I should like to retaliate by calling upon him to respond ; Mr. Asa W. Dickinson, of the legal profession, who now occupies a position in the Court of Jersey City.

Mr. Dickinson spoke as follows :

This is the first time that I ever heard of a fellow being made a goat ; possibly it is the first time I have ever, unwillingly, been made a goat. I think he must have a long score against me that he should commence at this late day to retaliate. It reminds me of a western trapper of whom I once heard, who had not been to church for a great many years ; he had not been to church for so long that he had got the formulas of the church and the proceedings of the theatres rather mixed in his mind. He appeared in a church on one Sunday, just when the minister was getting into the most impressive part of his sermon. The parson, or as we say in New Jersey, the dominie, had explained to the audience that upon the great judgment day, there would be a certain class who would be the sheep, and a certain class would be the goats. As the trapper came in, the preacher had asked, with a great deal of earnestness, "now, my brethren, upon that great day, which of you will be goat?" and paused for effect. Then he repeated the question, "who will be goat?" He paused again. Then he repeated the question again, "who will be goat?" The trapper, rising in the back part of the house, said, "wall, mister, rather than not see the play go on, I will be goat."

I suppose to bring this celebration to a successful close, it was necessary that somebody should be goat; and I was brought forward by my brother for that purpose. I am further reminded of a good young man down in New Jersey, who wanted to become a Methodist preacher; and he went to one of the old preachers, and said to him, "I am going to become a preacher, and I am going to the seminary to study." "Oh, no; you will never make a preacher," said the old man, "if you go there and study. If you want to be a preacher, go right up into the pulpit and preach; go right in next Sunday." "Yes," said the young man, "but I am afraid I must first study; I must first prepare myself before I can preach. Did you start that way?" "Certainly, I did; certainly, I did. That is the way I started, and that is the way you must start, if you want to be a successful preacher." "Well, tell me your experience," said the young man. "Well," said the old man, "the first Sunday that I preached, I went into the desk, and when it came sermon time, I looked my congregation in the face, and said, "Brethren, behold three things!" I repeated it: "Brethren, behold three things!" "Yes," said the young man, 'what did you do then?" "Well, I scratched round and looked along until I got three things for them to behold."

If I were to make a very extended speech this afternoon, I am afraid I should have to scratch round and look along to get three things for you to behold. I understand that there is to be a reception this evening, and of course, the younger members of the family—I do not count myself a young man; I am a good deal older than I look—have departed and will soon return dressed in their best bibs and tuckers, and show us, who are more venerable than they, how well dressed the daughters of Nathaniel and Mrs. Nathaniel can appear at a public reception; and I think it well that we should follow their example, that I cease talking, and that we should go to our homes and deck ourselves for this evening. I hope that my brother will be perfectly satisfied, and that he wont try to get square with me any more.

THE PRESIDENT—I am satisfied, but I will not speak for the rest of the request.

The following letters and telegrams were then read by the President:

"LARAMIE, WY. TER., August 8, 1883.
"To M. F. Dickinson:

"GREETINGS TO ALL THE DICKINSONS—May the objects of this meeting be fully attained, and all present enjoy themselves. Letter received too late to reply by mail. Am sorry to say press of business prevents my attendance.
"EDWARD DICKINSON."

[Mr. Dickinson is Superintendent of one of the divisions of the Union Pacific Railroad].

[*From Dr. Wm. Dickinson*].
"No. 1322 OLIVE ST.,
"ST. LOUIS, Mo., Aug. 6th, 1883.
"*Hon. M. F. Dickinson, Jr., President and Respected Kinsmen*—A voice from beyond the "Father of Waters"

sends to all sentiments of fraternal greeting. Personal presence being denied me, my spirit is with you on this commemorative occasion, and is in profound sympathy with the objects contemplated by it. In these and similar memorial occasions, I recognize the acknowledgement of the most pervasive and most potent conviction of the human mind, which, through all the ages, has found its grandest manifestation in uniting families and kindreds, in combining peoples and races, and in confederating even the remotest nations, which was emphasized by the teachings and exemplified in the life of our Saviour, viz.: *the fatherhood of God and the brotherhood of man.* And by them, also, humanity obtains a fresh baptism, and the apocalyptic millenium receives accumulative assurance of its complete realization.

"The public rehearsal and consideration of the virtues and deeds of our common ancestor will be barren of its best results, if from it we do not receive an inspiration that shall incite to nobler endeavor and higher achievement.

"May this convocation, therefore, by facilitating "a more intimate acquaintance with each other," multiply and strengthen the ties of our common family; awaken, cultivate and refine reciprocal sympathies, make us better men and women in our homes, more genial and helpful to our kindred, more influential for good to society, and more consecrated to the interests of patriotism and of humanity.

"The "Circular" received foreshadows the probability of "the early preparation and publication of a general genealogical history." Let this be done. It is a "consummation devoutly to be wished." Any assistance which I can lend for its accomplishment will be cheerfully rendered.

"I am, Very Respectfully, Your Kinsman,
"WILLIAM DICKINSON, M. D."

The audience then joined in singing the following hymn, by Mary E. Bullard, of Cambridge, Massachusetts:

TUNE—THE SWEET BYE AND BYE.

We have gathered from far and near,
   Through this land of the brave and the free,
To welcome with songs of good cheer
   A right happy company.

We shall think as we gather here,
   Of those who before us have trod ;
The fathers, to memory dear,
   At rest in the bosom of God.

They were men of the iron nerve ;
   They were men both pious and strong ;
They were men who could never swerve
   In their scorn and hatred of wrong.

Yea! they put their all at the stake
   In waging a pitiless strife ;
And for sweet humanity's sake
   They laid down their fortune and life.

O say! are we worthy such sires?
   Are we treading the paths that they trod?
Are we filled with like noble desires?
   Are we fighting for right and for God?

Let us gird on their armor to-day ;
   Let us shout with a three times three ;
Let us each most devoutly say,
   "God bless our dear family tree!"

The reading of letters was then resumed as follows:
[From Rev. Wm. C. Dickinson].

"LAFAYETTE, INDIANA, July 20, 1883.
"F. W. Dickinson, Esq.:

"DEAR SIR—I regret exceedingly that I cannot join personally in the approaching Dickinson reunion at Amherst, but distance and engagements will prevent.

"I have great pride in the name. It is good blood that has, so far back as we can trace it, run in the veins of the family.

"No part of our country has had a better reputation than the Connecticut Valley and the never fertile but always beautiful hills that inclose it east and west have had, for the substantial virtues of those who have dwelt there for two centuries past; and the Dickinsons, who have been a numerous and influential part of that population, have done their full part towards giving to that portion of Massachusetts its high reputation for the intelligence, thrift, sobriety and Christian character of its people. I hope some one will be appointed at this meeting to trace back their history and chronicle their deeds.

"The branch of the family to which I belong originated in Amherst.

"The old homestead is in the northern part of the town, and has been in possession of the family for now more than a century.

"My father was Rev. Baxter Dickinson, D. D.

"A good large number of our immediate kindred will be present. Among them one of my sisters, Miss Harriet A.

"Anything that you can send relative to the meeting will be highly appreciated.

"With warmest congratulations to the large and most worthy brotherhood, I am

"Very Truly Yours,
"WILLIAM C. DICKINSON."

[*From Henry W. Taft, Clerk of Courts of Berkshire County, Mass*].

"PITTSFIELD, August 4th, 1883.

"MY DEAR SIR—I was pleased to receive yours of the thirty-first and to find myself recognized as one of the Dickinson family. It is so long since I parted with the family *name* that I should have been slow to claim my rights of inheritance but for your kindly remembrance.

"I am quite proud of my descent from so many of the founders of Hadley. They were brave, earnest, God-fearing men, and among them there were many minds of superior intelligence and sagacity. As I read the scanty record of their lives, and by help of the imagination fill in the page with the not less truthful though unwritten story of their sacrifices and labors, I have come to look back to them over the two centuries which separate us with what I believe to be a just and reasonable feeling of filial reverence and affection.

"Our progenitor, Nathaniel Dickinson, was one of the leading and influential men both of Wethersfield and Hadley. He seems to have been much in the public service, and to have commanded the confidence and esteem of his fellow-townsmen. He was one of the pioneer settlers in Hadley, and it is not an unnatural inference from the record, that he was one of the Committee who laid out its broad and beautiful street, and so became entitled in this particular to the gratitude of succeeding generations. I am gratified to know that his descendants are inclined to do honor to his memory, and to meet to revive old associations, and extend their acquaintance with each other.

"It would give me much pleasure to be present at the gathering, but my engagements will not permit. If I do not presume too far, I should be glad, through you, to present my salutations to the brethren who will assemble on the eighth instant, and to say that I believe that the

Dickinson blood, which came to me through three generations of the name, still runs in my veins, and that I *cannot say* how much wiser and better I am for its presence.

"Yours Sincerely,
"HENRY W. TAFT.
"Hon. M. F. DICKINSON, Jr."

[*From Chas. Dickinson Adams*].

"NEW YORK, August 7th, 1883.

"MY DEAR DICKINSON—When I received your suggestion, that it would be peculiarly appropriate for me, on account of the Dickinson in my name, to gather with the Dickinson clan, at Amherst, and make a speech at the Dickinson dinner, I felt so much like doing it that I suspected there must be some Dickinson in my blood. Although I have owned the name for forty odd years, as did my father before me, and as does his grandson after me, I have never stopped to inquire how we became originally possessed of it. The truth is, my grandsire was a democrat, and,

> "Being not propped by ancestry,
> Whose grace chalks successors their way,"

I never dared look far behind him, lest I should fall upon a tory. But your letter encouraged me to secretly clamber up the Adams' genealogical tree, and I had no sooner got out on the big limb of my great grandfather, than I found grafted thereon, in the reign of George II, a Dickinson scion, one Sarah, daughter of Deacon Ebenezer Dickinson, of Amherst. Good wife Sarah ought to have insisted on having one of her children, at least, dubbed with the maternal cognomen. But blood will tell in the long run. The Adams boys married Dickinson girls right and left, and in due time, one begat a son, my father, whom they called Nathaniel Dickinson Adams.

after that Nathaniel Dickinson, familiarly known as "'Squire Nat," delegate from Amherst to the first Continental Congress, and, I suppose, after that still more famous Nathaniel Dickinson, who led his tribe up from Wethersfield into Hadley, in 1659, drove out the Wampanoags, and occupied the land.

"I had got thus far, when in came my youngest *brother, who calls himself a historian, prates about original research, pores over old church and town records, and dotes on moss-grown gravestones. He says that our great grandsire had two wives—not that he was a Mormon—but that his first wife, the aforesaid Sarah Dickinson, died, and was succeeded by one Grace Ward, who wrote poems and bore children of goodly number, from one of whom we are descended. So that, my brother says, there isn't a drop of Dickinson blood in a single corpuscle of my body. But, I refuse to believe this. It is only a way historians have of tilting well-settled historical facts, as when they try to prove that the Pilgrims never landed on Plymouth Rock, nor on the twenty-second of December. But, until it is shown on what they did land, I shall stick to it that I am a Dickinson, not only by name but by nature.

"Well, this whole subject of ancestry and posterity is a queer thing, and when you go into it there is no telling where you will come out. In Quincy, near Boston, stands a monument, sacred to the memory of one Henry Adams, who took his flight from the dragon persecution, in Devonshire, and alighted in 1634, with eight sons, near Mount Wollaston. One of them remained there, and was ancestor of a line of presidents, statesmen, and scholars. Another, hoping, I suppose, to better his and his children's fortunes, moved west, which was then bounded by the Connecticut river, and became the ancestor of a town constable and obscure highway surveyors, one of

* Prof. Herbert B. Adams, John Hopkins' University, Baltimore.

whom laid out a road from Lancaster to that river, and received a grant of one hundred and twenty-four acres of hard-scrabble in Roadtown, afterwards called Shutesbury. And while his—let us call him—tenth cousin, John Adams, and "The Illustrious Farmer," John Dickinson, of Pennsylvania, were revolutionizing the thirteen colonies, and laying the foundations of a mighty republic, he was trapping bears on the hills of Pelham and Shutesbury, and slyly stealing over Flat hills every Sunday night, ere sun-set, down to Amherst, to court Deacon Ebenezer Dickinson's fair daughter, Sarah, who, I insist upon it, at least for the time being, was my great grandmother.

I say you cannot always tell whither the study of your ancestry will take you. Sidney Smith said it would generally be to a scoundrel, and perhaps to the end of a rope. Seneca said that if we should trace our descent, we should find all slaves to come from princes, and all princes from slaves; fortune has so turned all things topsy-turvey in the long series of revolutions. But the origin of all mankind is the same; it is only a clear and a good conscience that makes a man noble, for that is derived from heaven itself.

> "What can ennoble sots or slaves or cowards?
> Alas! not all the blood of all the Howards."

But I must close. I fancy I see all the Dickinsons, and the sons of Dickinsons, flocking to-day to Amherst "as a cloud, and as the doves to their windows." The Kelloggs, and Eastmans, and Cowles and other natives are out on the hills, with their glasses.

Returning yesterday from St. Louis, I found the train loaded with Dickinsons. At Chicago more came on board. At Detroit a new car was added, and so on all the way to Albany. What a looking up of old furniture and family relics there will be! What consulting of old Bibles, and revival of old traditions!

If you find any stranger around Amherst this week with no Dickinson in his name, pity him; if he has none in his veins, references should be required; if he has none in either his name or his veins, there dwelleth not in him one good thing.

On the other hand, if he has Dickinson either in his name or blood, or, better still, in both, like you and me, let him exalt his horn and shout aloud for joy. He has something to swear by, and live for. And as "he takes pride in the noble achievements of remote ancestors," let him resolve to "achieve something himself, worthy to be remembered with pride by remote descendants."

Yours Sincerely,
CHARLES DICKINSON ADAMS.

The audience then joined in singing the last hymn on the program, written by Gideon Dickinson, M. D., of Milford, Massachusetts, and entitled

FAREWELL.

TUNE—HEBRON.

Now, as the parting hour draws near,
  Join we in one sad, closing song;
And ere we part forever here,
  Let us one final note prolong;
Then, as the fleeting years shall roll
  And bear us with time's tide along,
Often shall wake, within each soul,
  Some memory of our parting song.

Though we may wander far and wide,
  Never to meet on earth again,
Yet hearts by kindred blood allied
  Shall constant, to the last remain.

HYMN BY GIDEON DICKINSON.

And, wheresoe'er we chance to go,
   True as the needle to the pole,
Some unseen bond, in joy or woe,
   Shall link each kindred soul to soul.

Often may death and sorrow reign,
   And glowing hope sink down and die,
But kindred hearts in joy or pain,
   Shall own the force of kindred tie ;
And though in distant lands we roam,
   And though the deep between us rolls,
As our sad thoughts turn back to home
   True friendship shall unite our souls.

Many a lovely face and form,
   Seen here, in pride of youth, to-day,
Soon bowed by Fate's relentless storm,
   Stern Death's cold hand may sweep away ;
Yet summer flowers will often bloom,
   And these loved scenes will long remain,
But we, alas! this side the tomb,
   Shall nevermore all meet again.

As trembling tear-drops in the eye,
   Betray the secrets of the heart,
So doth, at times, a stifled sigh
   Reveal the pain it costs to part :
True as the needle to the pole,
   Let sigh and trembling tear-drop tell
That, here, each kindred heart and soul
   Now deeply feels—Farewell!—Farewell!

A song by Charles M. Dickinson of Binghamton, N. Y., entitled "Our Pioneers" was received too late to be printed in the program. We make room for the third and fourth stanzas:

The wild forest fell 'neath the axe's sharp knell;
  The spire pointed upward in place of the pine;
There the anthem was sung, there prayer found a tongue
  And blessings came down from the Father divine.
Soon all the land felt their resolute hand;
  The broad valleys blossomed which labor had won;
The hills rearing high bared their heads to the sky,
  And Holyoke uncovered looked up to the Sun.

Now, where log cabins stood in the opening wood,
  The swift spindles flash and the huge hammers ring;
Where they gathered to raise hymns of gladness and
    praise,
  A thousand sweet voices the same anthems sing;
All through the land, the beautiful land,
  Are voices of labor on every hand,
And each has a tone that is partly our own,
  For it honors the names of that patriot band.

After some announcements by the President, the meeting adjourned to meet at College Hall, at eight o'clock, for the Reception.

Promptly at that hour, College Hall was thronged with several hundred members of the Family, and several hours were occupied most delightfully, in forming acquaintances, tracing the branches of the Family tree, music and social intercourse. Kindred hearts seemed to readily respond to each other, and many of the acquaintances there formed will be remembered as among the pleasantest of a life-time.

THURSDAY'S PROCEEDINGS.

"AMHERST, MASS.,
"Thursday, August 9th, 1883.

Business meeting of the Dickinson Family.

Meeting called to order by M. F. Dickinson, Jr., of Boston, who stated briefly the proposal to form a permanent organization of the Dickinson Family and the objects of such an organization.

Moved, That we do form a permanent organization of the Dickinson Family, by the choice of such officers as may be thought necessary. Carried.

Moved, That M. F. Dickinson, Jr., of Boston, be the President of the Association. Carried.

Moved, That Francke W. Dickinson, of Springfield, Massachusetts, be the Secretary of the Association. Carried.

Moved, That the Secretary act as Treasurer also. Carried.

Moved, That the President appoint a committee to report a list of Vice-Presidents. Carried.

The President appointed as that committee Wharton Dickinson, Scranton, Pennsylvania; Augustus N. Currier, Worcester, Massachusetts; Henry C. Dickinson, San Francisco, California.

Moved, That the President and Secretary, with the following named gentlemen, viz.: George Montague, Amherst, Massachusetts; Austin Goodridge, Westminster, Vermont; Leonard A. Dickinson, Hartford, Connecticut; Dr. S. W. Dickinson, Marion, Virginia; and Edmund N. Dickinson, Amherst, Massachusetts, serve as Executive Committee. Carried.

Moved, That the following named gentlemen, viz.: Rev. Charles A. Dickinson, Lowell, Massachusetts; Wharton Dickinson, Scranton, Pennsylvania; Mahlon H. Dickinson, Philadelphia, Pennsylvania; Rev. Legh Richmond Dickinson, Great Bend, Pennsylvania, ; and Charles M. Dickinson, Binghamton, New York; serve as Historical Committee. Carried.

Moved, That the Executive Committee be charged with the duty of publishing the historical address of Rev. Charles A. Dickinson, and such portions of the rest of the exercises of the meetings, August 8th and 9th, 1883, as they see fit. Carried.

The committee appointed to report a list of names of Vice-Presidents, reported the following list, containing one from each branch of the family, viz.:

Massachusetts Dickinsons—Thomas A. Dickinson, Worcester, Massachusetts; Maryland Dickinsons—Samuel T. Dickinson, New York; Virginia Dickinsons—Judge Asa D. Dickinson, Springfield, Worsham Post-office, Prince Edwards County, Virginia; Pennsylvania Dickinsons—Hiram Corson, M. D., Plymouth Meeting, Pennsylvania; Scotch Dickinsons—Thomas Dickinson, Guilford, New York.

Moved, That the report be accepted, and the gentlemen named be the Vice-Presidents of the Association. Carried.

Moved, That James W. Dickinson, of West Hoboken, New Jersey, be added to the Vice-Presidents. Carried.

Moved, In view of the long, arduous and persevering labor expended by the Secretary, Francke W. Dickinson, of Springfield, Massachusetts, in behalf of the Dickinson

THURSDAY'S PROCEEDINGS. 149

meeting, that the members of this meeting tender to him their cordial, hearty and sincere thanks. Carried by a rising vote.

Moved, That we do now adjourn. Carried.

F. W. DICKINSON,
Secretary.

At the close of the Business Meeting, a large number of the Members of the Family took carriages and stages in waiting, for an excursion to Hadley and Mount Holyoke. At the Hadley Cemetery where Nathaniel Dickinson and his immediate descendants were buried, the following proceedings were had :

HADLEY CEMETERY, August 9th, 1883.

A number of the family, on the way to Mount Holyoke, stopped for a visit at this old burial place, and while here, it was

Moved, That the executive committee be requested to take measures to procure and erect upon the old family lot in Hadley burial ground, a suitable monument to the memory of Deacon Nathaniel Dickinson, one of the original settlers of Hadley, who died in 1676. Carried.

F. W. DICKINSON,
Secretary.

APPENDIX.

APPENDIX.

[Note 1.]

NATHANIEL DICKINSON.

Nathaniel Dickinson settled in Wethersfield 1637, and in the year 1645 he was elected Town Clerk, and was a Representative from 1646 to 1656. In 1659 he removed to Hadley, where he was chosen Freeman in 1661, and was Deacon and First Recorder. He changed his residence to Hatfield, Massachusetts, for a few years, and then returned to Hadley, where he died June 16, 1676. He married Anne ———, and by her had the following children :—first, Samuel, born July, 1638; second, Obadiah, born April 15, 1641; third, Nathaniel, born August, 1643; fourth, Nehemiah, born about 1644; fifth Hezekiah, born February, 1645; sixth, Azariah, born October 4, 1648, married Dorcas, slain in Swamp fight August 25, 1675; seventh, Thomas; eighth, Joseph; ninth John; tenth, Anna, or Hannah, who married (1) January 10 or June 16, 1670, John Clary; (2) Enos Kingsley, of Northampton.

[Note 2.]

All English authorities agree that John Dickenson, Alderman and Burgess of Leeds, was the first to bear the surname of Dickenson. Prior to that they simply went by their Christian names, viz.: Walter of Kenson, or William of Kenson, etc.

Wharton Dickinson.

[NOTE 3.]

This ancient coat of arms consisted of a gold cross between four hinds' heads, which were also of gold, the whole on a green field, with a hind's head in gold for a crest. The motto was, *Esse Quam Videri.* "To be rather than to appear." (See Sallust, Catiline, ch. LIV, for origin of this motto.)

The Dickinsons, of Cleypole, Lincolnshire, and Bradley, Staffordshire, had for a coat of arms: Azure, a fess between two lions *passant* ermine. Crest, *demi-lion rampant, per* pale ermine and azure.

Dickinson, Lord Mayor of London, 1757. His arms were: Azure, a *chevron* between three *croises formee, Or,* on a chief Argent, a *quatrefoil purpure.*

Dickinson, of King Weston: Arms, *Or a bend,* engrailed between two lions *rampant,* gules.

Dickinson, of Abbott Hill: Arms, quarterly first and fourth gules, a fess ermine between two lions *passant.* Crest, out of cloud, a cubit arm holding a branch of laurel *vert.*

[NOTE 4.]

BRANCHES FROM SYMON AND CATHERYNE DICKENSON.

About 1575 Symon Dickenson, of Bradley, Staffordshire, married Catheryne, only daughter of Hon. Geoffrey Dudley, second son of Edward, fifth Lord Dudley, and had three sons—First, Edward; second, William; third, Charles.

First—Edward Dickenson, of Bradley, married Joyce Fowke, of Braewood. Line now supposed extinct.

Second—Rev. William Dickenson, D.D., rector Appleton and Besseleigh, near Oxford, married Mary, daughter of Edmund Colepepper, Esq., and had five children—First,

Edmund; second, Francis; third, William; fourth, John; fifth, Elizabeth.

First branch—Edmund, M. D., of London, first son of William, of Appleton, physician to King Charles II., died April, 1707, aged eighty-three, leaving by his wife, Elizabeth Laddington, an only daughter, Elizabeth, married first, to Sir G. Shires, and second, to Baron Blomberg.

I. JAMAICA DICKINSONS.

Second Branch.—Francis, second son of William of Appleton, of Barton, Jamaica, born in 1632, married in 1662, Mary, daughter of Stephen Crook, and dying in England in 1704, left—first, Jonathan; second, Caleb, who returned to England; third, Benjamin.

First—Jonathan Dickinson was born in the Island of Jamaica, West Indies, about 1675. He married there Mary, sister to Colonel Gale, and in 1699, through the persuasions of Samuel Carpenter and Isaac Norris, came to Philadelphia. Here he soon became a successful merchant and a prominent public man. He was Clerk of the Assembly in 1698; Member of Assembly, 1710, 1716, 1718, 1719; Provincial Councillor, 1711 and 1722; Mayor of Philadelphia, 1712, 1717, 1719; Associate Judge of Supreme Court, 1715, 1718; Justice of the Peace, 1718; Master in Chancery, 1720. Jonathan Dickinson owned "The Vineyard," one thousand two hundred and thirty acres, part of Spingetsburg manor, Philadelphia County. He was one of the eight gentlemen of the province of Pennsylvania who owned a four-wheel coach. He died in 1722, leaving—first, Jonathan, who married Rachael Humes, a Quakeress, of Rhode Island, where he died childless in 1727; second, Joseph, who joined his uncle Caleb in England, where he married and had one daughter; third, John, who died unmarried; fourth, Mary, married Francis Jones, of Rhode Island, but left no issue; fifth, Hannah, who married Thomas Masters and had Thomas; died in infancy.

Third branch—William of Abingdon, third son of William of Appleton, had—first, Thomas; second, William.

II. AYRSHIRE DICKINSONS.

First, Thomas of Abingdon married Jane, daughter of Moses Thirkeld, of Lancashire; removed about 1670 to Ayrshire, Scotland, between Ayr and Catrine, and left—first, Moses; second, Thomas; third, Josiah.

These three brothers in 1690 landed in Boston, and settled in Deerfield, afterwards in Hatfield, Massachusetts.

First—From Moses descended David, or David Ebenezer, who married Sarah, great-granddaughter of Governor John Winslow. He removed to Milton, Litchfield County, Connecticut, and left issue—first, Oliver; second, Reuben. Reuben married Sarah Gibbs, but left no issue. Oliver married Mary Kirkham Palmerlee, and had issue—first, Oliver, born 1757; second, Solomon, born 1759; third, Mary, born 1762; fourth, David, born 1766; fifth, Sarah, born 1768; sixth, Daniel, born 1772; seventh, Abel, born 1774; eighth, Desire, born 1785.

Oliver, jr., married Anna, daughter of Daniel Landon, and had issue—first, Anson, born 1779, whose adopted children are William Dickinson and Mary Anne, widow of Honorable Truman Smith; second, Raphael, born 1781, and had issue—first, Sarah; second, Elizabeth; third, Leonard. Third—Ambrose, born 1783; fourth, Lucinda, born 1785, who left Mary Anne; fifth, Leonard, born about 1788; sixth, Henry, born 1791, left Edwin; seventh, Anna; eighth, Daniel, born 1795; ninth, Anna Landon, born 1798; tenth, Andrew, born 1801, father of Legh

Richmond and Helen Catlin Gesner and grandfather of Irving and May Dickinson, and of Richmond, and Anthon Gesner.

Solomon left by his first wife, Anna, Amos, Andros and Harvey. After her death he removed to Pennsylvania, and by his second wife left numerous descendants in that State, and in New York. Mary married John Bissell. David left David and Roxana. Sarah married Daniel Landon, brother of Anna, wife of Oliver second. Abel left Alphonso, Letitia and Amanda. Desire married Daniel Hall, and left three sons, William, Norman and Salmon, and four daughters, Lucy, Mary, Sally and Janet.

Second—From Thomas, descended Thomas, ancestor of Daniel S. and his children.

Third—Of Josiah, no record remains.

Thomas the second of the brothers from Scotland, had a son and grandson of the same name. The third Thomas was born about 1725. He settled at Hatfield, below Amherst, in Hampshire County, Massachusetts. He also left a son Thomas, who married Anne Stevens, of Hatfield. He removed to Salem, on the Waterbury river, New London County, Connecticut. He had issue—first, Anne, born about 1769; second, Thomas, born about 1771; third, Samuel, born about 1773; fourth, Daniel T., born about 1775; fifth, John, born about 1777; sixth, Charles, born about 1779; seventh, Nathaniel, born about 1781.

Thomas, John, Charles and Nathaniel, removed first to Norfolk, Litchfield County, Connecticut, and about 1805 removed to Genesee County, New York. Large numbers of their descendants are to be found in Buffalo, Geneva, Rochester, Syracuse, and neighboring places. Andrew B. Dickinson, U. S. Minister to Nicaragua, who died 1873, belonged to this branch. Anne Dickinson married William Hubbard and had Samuel Dickinson, born 1799, died 1865, M. C. from Connecticut. Samuel Dickin-

158   APPENDIX.

son (second son) married, and had—first, Samuel ; second,
Anne, who married Richard Hubbard, of Hamden, and
had—first, Richard, born 1814, M. C. from Connecticut,
Governor Connecticut 1877-1878 ; second, Chester, born
1818, M.C. from Connecticut. Daniel Tompkins married
Mary Caulkins (Hoadley) of Salem, and in 1798 removed
to Goshen, twenty miles north-east of Salem, where he
cleared off a new farm, but in 1807 he removed to
Chenango County, New York, and settled at Guilford.
He had—first, Erastus ; second, John R. ; third, Thomas
of Guilford, New York ; fourth, Daniel Stevens ; fifth,
Ellen ; sixth, Martin ; seventh, Pomona.

LONDON AND LEEDS DICKINSONS.

Second—William of London, second son of William
of Abingdon, married Judith Dickinson, and had—first,
Thomas ; second, Nathaniel ; third, Mary ; fourth, Jane.

Fourth branch—John of Leeds and London, fourth son
of William of Appleton, married Mary Rutter and had—
first, John ; second, Judith, wife of William of London.

Fifth branch, Elizabeth, fifth child of William of
Appleton, was married to Right Rev. Richard Sterne,
D.D., Archbishop of York.

III. VIRGINIA DICKINSONS.

Third—Charles of London, third son of Symon and
Catheryne Dickenson, married Rachael Carter, and dying
in 1633, left—first, Walter ; second, Henry ; third, John.
All three came to Virginia in 1654. Walter, in 1660,
settled near Trappee, Talbot County, Maryland, where he
died, 1681. By Jane Yarrett he left William Dickenson,
who married Elizabeth Powell, and dying in 1717, left
Samuel, who by Judeth Troth, his first wife, left, in 1760,
Henry, who left Samuel, who left Samuel S., who left
Samuel, who left Samuel T. ; by Mary Cadwalader, his

second wife. Samuel left Governor John Dickinson, of Delaware and Pennsylvania, and General Philemon, of New Jersey.

NEW JERSEY DICKERSONS.

Walter Dickinson, or Dickerson, as his decendants claim the name should be spelt, settled in Hepburn, Essex, and had several children. A great-grandson of his (for such he claimed to be), Philemon, left England in 1638 to escape the persecutions of Laud and the High Church party. In 1641 he was admitted a freeholder of Salem, Massachusetts. In 1645 he removed to Southold, Suffolk County, Long Island, where he died in 1672. By his will of June 20, 1665, he divided his property between his wife Mary, his sons Thomas and Peter, and his daughters Elizabeth and Mary. By the records in the Surrogate's Office, New York, it will be seen that administration papers were granted to his widow, October 28, 1672. His son Peter was born in Southold 1657; married a daughter of Thomas Reeve, from whom, in 1707, he received a valuable real estate. He died in 1724 (the year of his son Peter's birth), leaving issue—First, John; second, Thomas, jr., who remained on Long Island; third, Joshua; fourth, Elizabeth; fifth, Daniel; sixth, Mary; seventh, Catherine; eighth, Peter, jr. Thomas, Joshua, Daniel and Peter, in 1745, removed to Morris County, New Jersey. A son of Daniel removed to Seneca County, New York, in 1795. He has a large issue living in that region, one of whom, Gamaliel, seems to have obtained quite a reputation.

Thomas Dickerson, jr., had a son John, who had in turn David, who married a Miss Bailey and had—first, Bailey; second, Mahlon; third, Sylvester; fourth, Rachael; fifth, Caroline, married Mr. Bentley, of Morristown; sixth, Jane, married Johnson, of Nashville, Tennessee; seventh, Margaret, married William Gordon, of Newark,

New Jersey. David had a sister, Phœbe, who married William Ford, of Rockaway, New Jersey.

Rachael Dickerson married Alfred Powers, of Phœnixville, Pennsylvania, and had—first, Freeman; second, George; third, Alfred of Scranton, Pennsylvania; fourth, Henry; fifth, Lucius, of Scranton, Pennsylvania; sixth, Elizabeth; seventh, David.

Thomas, the eldest son of Philemon Dickerson, of Long Island, had a son Walter, who came to New Jersey in 1761; he had a son Noohdiah, who died recently, over eighty.

Joshua, the second son of the elder Peter and brother of Daniel and Thomas, jr., was great-grandfather of the Hon. Isaac N. Dickerson, of Cumberland County, New Jersey, ex-Member of Congress.

Peter was a member of the First Provincial Congress of New Jersey, and in 1776 raised a company which was joined to the First Regiment of Maxwell's Brigade, in which capacity he did good service. He died in 1780, leaving—first, Jonathan; second, Philemon, who had first, Caleb, who had two sons, Samuel T. and Caleb. Samuel T. had two sons, George F. and Samuel T. Caleb had one son, Joseph, of Ohio.

Jonathan was born September 20, 1747, and died in 1805, leaving—first, Silas, died unmarried, in 1833; second, Governor Mahlon, of New Jersey, born 1769, died at Morristown, New Jersey, October 5, 1853, never married; third, John, M. D., of Chester, Pennsylvania, who left (1) Mahlon H., a lawyer of some note in Philadelphia; fourth, Sylvester; fifth, Peter; sixth, Caroline, married F. D. Canfield and had (1) Rev. Frederick D., (2) Augustus C., Member of New Jersey Legislature; seventh, Rebecca, died unmarried; eighth, Margaret, married Lewis Cass, Esq., of Pittsburg, and had (1) General George W. Cass, of Pittsburg; ninth, Isaac; tenth, Governor Philemon, of New Jersey, born 1792, died December

10, 1862, at Trenton, and had (1) John Henry, (2) Philemon, (3) Edward, the famous patent lawyer; tenth, Mary, married John M. Gould, of Paterson, New Jersey.

[NOTE 6.]

WILL OF SIR GILBERT GRAFTON.

The following is from the last will and testament of Sir Gilbert Talbot, of Grafton, the younger, grandfather of Mrs. Symon Dickenson. It bears date, October 19, 1542:

"He orders his body to be buried in the Chapel of St. John the Evangelist, adjoining the parish church of White Church, in the County of Salop, and a tomb of marble to be laid on him; and that four banners be carried at his sepulture; one of the Trinity, another of the Annunciation of Our Lady, the third of St. John the Evangelist, and the fourth of St. Anthony. And he bequeaths a torch and three shillings four pence to every church his body come by. Also, that his executors found a perpetual charity within the said chapel, and pray for his soul, the soul of his father (Sir Gilbert Talbot, the elder), his mother's soul, and other of his ancestors' souls; and the priest who performed these masses was to receive five pounds sterling as his wages, to be levied of his lands and tenements in White Church.

"AND, WHEREAS, Sir Gilbert Talbot, his father, deceased, left one gown of cloth of gold, one robe of black velvet (used for the Order of the Garter), one table of timber for the altar in said chapel, one image of Our Lady, the Virgin, and four images of wood, and one book lined with gold, to be used within the said chapel; he now wills that they be kept in a coffer for the use before limited. He wills to his wife, Dame Elizabeth

Talbot (his second wife, and widow of George Aynton, Esq., when he married her), all the jewels she had at her espousals; as, also, legacies to his daughters, Margaret, wife of Robert Newport, Esq.; Elizabeth, wife of John Littleton, Esq.; Eleanor, wife of Geoffrey Dudley, Esq. (parents of Catheryne Dickenson), and Mary Talbot. To his eldest son, Humphrey Talbot, he bequeaths his manor of Longford; and to his son, Walter Talbot, lands in the City of Worcester. To his grandsons, the Littletons, and his nephews, the Talbots, he leaves twenty shillings each. He constitutes as his executors, his son, Humphrey Talbot, of Longford; his brother, Sir John Talbot, of Abbington; and his spiritual overseer and right good lord, the Bishop of Worcester."

This will was proved in November, 1542, showing that Sir Gilbert made it on his dying bed.

Another point is also established by the will, and that is the date of the marriage of Eleanor Talbot and Geoffrey Dudley. This marriage must have occurred within a year prior to Sir Gilbert's death, as they had, as yet, no issue, else legacies would have been left to this issue. From this we infer that their only son, Thomas, of Russels, was born in 1543, and their only daughter, Catheryne, in 1545. This lady was married to Symon Dickenson about 1575, as that is the date of the grant of the Dudley Dickenson arms.

"Russels" and "Dudley Castle," the seats of the Lords Dudley and Bradley, the seats of the Dickensons, were all within five miles of one another; as were, also, Renkridge and Braewood, from the first of which William Dickenson, of Bradley, took his wife, Rachael King, and from the second of which Edward of Bradley, took his wife, Joyce Fowke.

For an interesting description of Castle Dudley, built by Dud the Saxon, as early as A. D. 700, see Hugh Miller's First Impressions of England, chapter V.

[NOTE 7.]

DANIEL S. DICKINSON.

Daniel Stevens, son of Daniel T. and Mary Caulkins Dickinson, was born in the town of Goshen, Connecticut, September 11th, 1800. He was the fourth of a family of eight children. In 1806 the family removed to Chenango County, New York, and settled in the town of Guilford. Here the subject of this sketch passed his youth mostly in the hardy and laborious occupations of the farm. The country was new, and the parents possessed and instilled into their children those industrious, self-reliant, manly qualities which took deep root in the nature of Daniel S., and formed the foundation of his subsequent greatness and power.

His early educational advantages were meagre, but he acquired a thorough practical education, and having aptitude for study and a fine literary taste, he pursued a system of self-education and extensive reading that soon made him well versed in the classics, in poetry, history, the various branches of science and general literature. He remembered what he read and quoted from ancient and modern writers with surprising fertility, felicity and effect.

About the age of seventeen Daniel S. was apprenticed to a cloth-dresser and became well-skilled in the trade, though he never pursued it to any extent after serving his apprenticeship.

From 1820 to 1825 his time was mainly occupied in teaching, and he also commenced the study of law. He was admitted to the bar in 1828, and commenced practicing law in Guilford, but seeking a more extensive field for business, he removed to Binghamton, New York, in 1831, and resided there until the date of his death. In 1836, he was elected to the New York State Senate, where he at once took high rank among the leading legislators of that body. At the close of his term in 1840, the Democratic State Convention nominated him for Lieutenant-Governor. He was defeated, though receiving five thousand more votes than the Democratic Presidential ticket. In 1842 he was again nominated for Lieutenant-Governor and elected.

In 1844 he was appointed to fill a vacancy in the United States Senate, and in 1845 he was elected for a full term as his own successor. For several years he was Chairman of the Committee on Finance, and took a leading part in all the prominent measures before Congress during his term of service, which embraced some of the most eventful years of the national history. A resolution offered by him in the Senate in December, 1847, was the first public enunciation of "Popular Sovereignty," and the doctrine thus put forth was finally made the basis of the compromise measures of 1850.

In 1852 Mr. Dickinson was a delegate to the Democratic National Convention at Baltimore, and here occurred an incident which well illustrated his sharp sense of honor and the sterling qualities of his character. The Convention had balloted for four days without result. It was conceded that Virginia held the key to the situation. On the fifth day, the Virginia delegation nominated and voted solidly for Mr. Dickinson amid much enthusiasm. He was a delegate for General Cass. As Cass was still a candidate, Mr. Dickinson did not think it honorable to permit his name to be placed in nomination. He firmly and promptly declined the proffered honor. Virginia then brought forward the name of Franklin Pierce, and he was nominated and elected.

In 1853 Mr. Dickinson was appointed Collector of the Port of New York, but declined the appointment. From the close of his service in the Senate until 1861, he devoted himself to his profession, with conspicuous success. His noble and patriotic devotion to his country upon the breaking out of the Rebellion, is too well remembered to need extensive reference. Though he had been an earnest Democratic partisan for many years, he quickly cast off party ties and threw his whole heart, his great influence and commanding talents into the cause of the Union. His prompt action and eloquent speeches were very effective in breaking up party lines and uniting the North for the suppression of the Rebellion.

The political campaign of 1861 took shape in the formation of a Union party, and Mr. Dickinson naturally became one of its leaders. He was nominated for the highest office then about to become vacant, that of Attorney General, and elected by one hundred thousand majority.

In 1863, he was tendered an appointment as Judge of the New York Court of Appeals, but declined it. In 1865 President Lincoln appointed him United States Attorney for the Southern District of New York, which office he accepted, and was discharging its duties when he died suddenly in New York, April 12th, 1866.

In 1822, Mr. Dickinson married Lydia Knapp, a most lovely and admirable woman. Four children, one son and three daughters, blessed that union, two of whom, Mrs. Lydia L. D. Courtney, of New York, and Mrs. Mary S. D. Mygatt, of Brooklyn, still survive. Mrs. Mygatt and family attended the Amherst Reunion.

Though Mr. Dickinson won conspicuous position in National affairs, it was in the home circle that his greatness appeared to the best advantage. The domestic virtues bore their richest fruit in his character. In all his social relations he was most genial and winning, and his popularity in the city where he lived, was so great that when he died, the expressions of sorrow were as profound and universal as if death had entered every home.

[NOTE 8.]

Philemon, Salem, tanner, came with Benjamin Cooper, of Brampton County, Suffolk, as one of his servants. Embarked May 10, 1637, in the Mary Ann, from Yarmouth; had grant of land 1637; administrator of the church 1641; freeman, June 2, 1641; married Mary, daughter of Thomas Payne, of Salem; had baptised there Mary, March 20, 1642; Thomas, March 10, 1644; Elizabeth. Recorded as freeman of Connecticut, but his will was proved in New York, where his widow was made administrator October 28, 1672. This name uniform with Dickerson in New York, recorded as it is found in Augmentation Office, Westminster Hall, on the return from custom house at Yarmouth, but the name at baptism is spelt Feleman.—*Savage's Genealogy, New England*

[NOTE 9.]

GOVERNOR MAHLON DICKERSON.

Mahlon Dickerson, whose ancestor Philemon came from England to Salem, Massachusetts, in 1638, and thence removed in 1645, to Suffolk County, Long Island, was the grandson of Peter Dickerson, who in 1745 removed from Long Island to Morris County, New Jersey, and the second son of Jonathan Dickerson. He was Quartermaster General of Pennsylvania; Recorder of Philadelphia; Attorney General of Pennsylvania; Member of New Jersey Legislature; Associate Judge of Supreme Court of New Jersey; Governor of New Jersey, and United States Senator for seventeen years, 1817 to 1834; Secretary of the Navy from 1834 to 1838; United States District Judge; President of American Institute. He was born in 1769, and died at Morristown, New Jersey, October 5, 1853. He was never married.

APPENDIX.   167

[Note 10.]
Governor Philemon Dickerson.

Philemon, tenth son of Peter and brother of Governor Mahlon Dickerson, was born 1792, and died December 10, 1862, at Trenton, New Jersey. He was Member of Congress from New Jersey from 1833 to 1835, and again from 1839 to 1841; Governor of New Jersey from 1836 to 1837. In 1842 he succeeded his brother as United States District Judge, holding the office until his death.

[Note 11.]
President Jonathan Dickinson.

Jonathan, son of Hezekiah, fifth of Nathaniel's children, and of Abigail, daughter of Samuel Blackman, of Stratford, was born at Hatfield, Massachusetts, April 22, 1688. His father was a merchant in Hatfield. He graduated at Yale College 1706; in 1708 was ordained a Presbyterian minister, and settled at Elizabeth, New Jersey. He preached regularly to six or seven congregations. He not only exerted a permanent influence in building up churches, but was an acknowledged leader in the old synod of Philadelphia, and, subsequently, in the synod of New York. Although sound in the doctrines of the Westminster confession, he firmly opposed the binding authority of uninspired confessions and creeds. He was prominent in the formation of the synod of New York. He warmly espoused Indian missions, and was instrumental in founding and securing a charter for Nassau Hall (Princeton College). He was elected President, but only lived to perform the duties a single year. Dr. Gillett (History Presbyterian Church, I, 40) characterizes him as a man of "rare sagacity, calm judgment and unshrinking firmness." Dr. John Erskine said that the British Isles had not produced any writers on divinity, in the eighteenth century, equal to Dickinson and Jonathan Edwards. He died October 17, 1747. (*c. Schaff-Herzog Encyclopædia; Sprague's Annals; Judd's History of Hadley, arranged by L. M. Boltwood, of Amherst.*)

[NOTE 12.]

There seems to be good reason for believing that Nathaniel was buried in the old Hadley burying ground, near the grave of his descendant, Nehemiah.

[NOTE 13.]

Samuel was the ancestor of a large number of the Amherst Dickinsons. His son Ebenezer, born February 2, 1684, married Hannah Frary, and had eight children. Nathan (or Nathaniel), son of Ebenezer, born May 30, 1712, moved from Hatfield to Amherst in 1742, and built the house on East street, which is now standing. He had three wives and three sets of children—fourteen in all. By Thankful Warner he had, Nathan, born October 19, 1695; Ebenezer, born January 3, 1741; Irene, born July 13, 1743; Enos, born March 28, 1746. By Joanna Leonard, of Springfield, he had, Azariah, born March 6, 1752; Elihu, born October 14, 1753; Shelah, born September 20, 1755; Thankful, born March 15, 1758; Lois, baptised August 5, 1759; Asa, born May 10, 1761; Levi; Joanna, baptised April 6, 1766. By Judith Hosmer he had Stephen, baptised July 6, 1770.

[NOTE 14.]

REV. TIMOTHY DICKINSON.

Timothy was the eldest of eight children of Nathan and Esther Dickinson. His father, who died August 3, 1825, aged ninety, was one of the first settlers of Amherst. For seventy years he was a member of the Church of Christ, and was "a kind neighbor, a warm friend, and affectionate in all the relations of life." His mother was Esther Fowler, of Westchester, Connecticut. She was in sympathy with all best things, and trained her children to obedience, loyalty to duty and self-reliance.

At sixteen, Timothy joined the American army at Ticonderoga, serving his country as a soldier for fifteen months. He prepared for college at Northampton, under Dr. Dwight, afterward president of Yale College; was graduated at Dartmouth in 1785, and appointed preceptor of Moore's Charity School, connected with the college. He studied theology with Rev. David Tappan, minister at Newbury, Massachusetts, and at Hopkinton, New Hampshire, and was settled at Holliston, Massachusetts, Dr. Tappan preaching his ordination sermon, February 18, 1789.

In November he married Margaret, daughter of Rev. Joshua Prentiss, who was for forty-two years pastor in Holliston.

The following inscription marks the stone over his grave:

"Rev. Timothy Dickinson, A. M.
"He was twenty-four years pastor of the Church of Christ,
"in this town.
"He was born at Amherst, in this state,
"June 25, 1761.
"Died July 6, 1813. Age LII."

"He was interesting and beloved in all his relations of life, constant in his exertions to do good, and ardent in his desire for the prosperity of Zion. As a preacher he was animated, pungent and evangelical. He zealously defended the faith once delivered to the saints, and faithfully taught the distinguishing doctrines of the gospel. He lived as he died, an example of what he taught."

Dr. Emmons, in his discourse delivered at the funeral, says: "Nature endowed Mr. Dickinson with that placid countenance, those social virtues and mental excellences which attracted the love and esteem of all. He was very apparently the man of God, who exhibited the reality and beauty of religion in his private conversation, as well as in his public and official conduct. He had a clear, strong and pleasant voice, which enabled him to speak with peculiar propriety and energy."

Rev. Mr. Adams, in his historical discourse, wrote: "An aged member of this church, who remembers Mr. Dickinson, says 'he was very social and lively. I never had an idea or heard that he had a failing.'"

Of himself, he wrote in his diary: "I have got into the habit of doing almost everything I do by extraordinary effort. When I read, I do it with dispatch. When I write, I am obliged to accomplish so much in such a time. When I journey, the rain must be very hard to hinder my progress. I am ever engaged in the object before me.

"I can differ from a benevolent man and not shun his house, and so can he from me.

"I am very much disgusted with neutrals. Let the truth come out. Let men not be ashamed to appear what they are."

He published several occasional sermons, one of which was preached in 1811, before the Massachusetts Missionary Society, of which he was one of the founders.

[NOTE 15]

GOVERNOR JOHN DICKINSON.

John Dickinson, of Dover, Delaware, was born at "Croise-dore," the seat of his father, Judge Samuel Dickinson, near Trappe, Talbot County, Maryland, No-

GOVERNOR JOHN DICKINSON. 171

vember 8, 1732. His mother was Mary Cadwalader, of Philadelphia. After studying law in Philadelphia, he spent three years at the Temple, in London; he returned to America and practiced in Philadelphia. He was member of Delaware Assembly 1760, of Pennsylvania Assembly from 1762 to 1776, and of the General Congress 1765; Member of the First Revolutionary Congress in 1774, and a member in subsequent years. In June, 1776, he opposed the Declaration of Independence, when the motion was considered by Congress, because he doubted the policy of that particular measure, "without some preliminary trial of our strength," and before the terms of Confederation were settled and foreign assistance made certain. Within a few days after the Declaration, he was, however, *the only* member of Congress who marched to face the enemy. He accompanied his regiment to Elizabeth Town in July, to repel the invading enemy, and he remained there until the end of the time of service. In 1779, he was member of Congress from Delaware, and in 1781 was President, or Governor of Delaware. In 1782 he was chosen Captain-General and Commander-in-chief in and over the Commonwealth of Pennsylvania, and remained in office from November, 1782, to October, 1785. In 1783, with Benjamin Rush and others, he founded the college at Carlisle, Pennsylvania, which was named by the Legislature of the State, Dickinson College. From 1783 to his death, he was President of the Board of Trustees. He died, 1808, aged 75 years.

In November, 1767, he began to publish his celebrated letters against the acts for taxation of the Colonies, in which writing he supported the liberties of his country, and contributed much toward the American Revolution. Of the eloquent and important State papers issued by the First Congress, he wrote the principal ones. His political writings were published in two volumes, 8vo, 1801. He was the acknowledged author of the system of electing United States Senators by the State Legislatures. *For full account of John Dickinson's life and public services, see article by* Wharton Dickinson, *in Magazine of American History, September, 1883.*

[NOTE 16.]

HON. SAMUEL FOWLER DICKINSON.

Samuel Fowler, the youngest son, and seventh of the eight children of Nathan and Esther (Fowler) Dickinson, was born in Amherst, Massachusetts, October 19, 1775. He was trained by the same maternal hand as his brother, and with like results of character and piety. Gentle and sensitive, and with more than ordinary mental gifts, he was one of the best beloved in his home by brothers and sisters, and was encouraged by his parents to follow his taste for study. After instruction by Judge Strong of Amherst, he entered Dartmouth College at sixteen, and maintaining high rank as a scholar, graduated in 1815 with the second honor, of Latin salutatorian. Accepting an invitation to become principal of the Academy at New Salem, he taught one year with marked success, but a severe illness overtaking him, and working a hope for his spiritual life, changed his plan of work. Uniting with the Congregationalist Church, he was elected a deacon at twenty-one, and for forty years "filled the office well." He began the study of theology with his brother Timothy at Holliston. Between these brothers there was an affinity and love like that of David and Jonathan, and he was watched over with parental tenderness. But he needed a more active life, and entered the law office of his former teacher, Judge Strong, and having completed his legal studies, began the practice of his profession in his native town. His success was so great that it is said "he *did* more business than *all* the lawyers in Hampshire County."

The magnetism of his nature attracted friends and placed him in offices of trust and of leadership. For fifteen years, from 1804 to 1818, he was Town Clerk of Amherst. In 1827 he was chosen a Representative to the State Legislature, or "General Court," and again as Senator. He never disappointed the trust reposed in him by falsity of word or deed.

In 1802 he was married to Lucretia Gunn, of Amherst. The romance of their marriage would be interesting to relate. Five sons and four daughters gave these parents heavy responsibilities of education and training. The need of wider facilities for education prompted him, with others, to establish Amherst Academy. A building, apparatus and the best teachers were secured at large outlay, making it one of the best schools in the state. Young men needing aid in obtaining an education were always encouraged and assisted by his liberality.

Samuel Fowler Dickinson was chief and foremost in founding Amherst College. He was one of the three men to whose exertions, through opposition and discouragement, this institution owes its existence. He expended time, labor, influence and money to bring about this result, and after years of conflict saw his perseverance crowned with success. The number of ministers and missionaries it has sent forth, greater in proportion to its size and age than any other College in the country, is the answer to his prayer. Upon its walls over his name might be inscribed, "*Si monumentum requiris, circumspice.*"

In his family and in public life he gave proof that a Christian is the "highest style of man." "An excellent spirit was in him." His large-heartedness and desire to help those in need sometimes overtaxed his judgment, and his name was often endorsed on notes to a large amount, which he was obliged to furnish the money for, while several men thus helped lived in affluence on his bounty, without recognizing the source. His public spirit was shown in planting trees by the highway. When asked what benefit this would be to him, he would reply, "Somebody will be benefited if not I."

He allowed himself but four hours of sleep, studying and reading till midnight, and rising at four o'clock he often walked to Pelham or some other town before breakfast. Going to court at Northampton, he would catch up his green bag and walk the whole seven miles. "*I cannot wait to ride,*" he would say to those who suggested that many horses in his stable would be idle, and outwalked the stage, with its four-in-hand, to Northampton. Bread, cheese and coffee, apples and old cider before breakfast were almost his sole diet. No man could outwork him, mentally or physically. He was ill but once in many years, till his last sickness of one week.

The loving daughter, who has traced these outlines of her noble father, says: "I never saw him laugh but once, yet he was always cheerful and genial; always had the right word in the right place for every one, and could make himself agreeable to all classes of men, showing his appreciation of every effort."

[NOTE 17.]

REV. AUSTIN DICKINSON.

Austin, the son of Azariah and Mary (Eastman) Dickinson, and an elder brother of Baxter Dickinson, D. D., was born in Amherst, Massachusetts, February 19, 1791. He belonged to the sixth generation of Nathaniel's descendants. His mother was eminently pious, wise and faithful, and deeply impressed these qualities upon her son.

He graduated with honor from Dartmouth College in 1813. Though laboring under great disadvantages from infirm health and consequent religious depression, he was remarkable in all branches of study. He was a deep thinker and a strong, original writer.

After several years spent in study, travel and teaching, he was licensed to preach by the North Association, of Hartford, Connecticut, February 2, 1819. His imperfect health preventing his accepting a pastorate, he traveled in the North and South, preaching and visiting colleges, seminaries and churches, forming missionary societies, establishing schools, organizing Bible and tract distributions, and promoting circulation of religious periodicals.

In 1821, through his instrumentality, $35,000 were obtained for Maryville College, Tennessee; and in 1822, $30,000 for Amherst College, and $50,000 for her charity fund, were secured, under his agency. In this work, and in procuring a charter against strong opposition, he continued two years. Dr. Humphrey, president of the college, said: "Mr. Dickinson brought influence to bear upon the public mind which few men could have wielded, and for which the college is more indebted than one in a hundred of its friends is aware of."

As a preacher Mr. Dickinson excited great attention at the very commencement of his career. There was an imposing magnificence in his style, a grandeur in his imagery, and a calm but impressive solemnity of voice and utterance, which produced a sublime, sombre eloquence, that possessed for every intellectual listener an inexpressible charm.

On April 19, 1826, Mr. Dickinson was ordained an evangelist, at Amherst, and soon after entered upon his next enterprise, the improvement of the American pulpit. To this end he established *The National Preacher*, which soon attained great popularity. He devoted his time and his income to the advancement of benevolent institutions, denying himself even the ordinary comforts of life, that he might have more to give.

In 1831 he visited England for health, attended many pastoral meetings, preaching to many congregations. During this tour he carefully informed himself respecting the educational and benevolent organizations of Great Britain, and made many valuable acquaintances.

In 1844 he commenced the crowning work of his life, the introduction of religious intelligence into secular papers. Much tact was necessary in this enterprise, and for over five years he labored with increasing results, attending in all parts of the country, religious anniversaries and conventions, and furnishing simultaneous reports to the leading papers of the United States, working night and day with untiring energy in this great enterprise. Overtaxed by his exertions, he was seized with cholera in New York, while resting in the family of his brother, and died August 15, 1849, in the midst of enlarged plans for advancing the Redeemer's kingdom. He was buried at Amherst, and friends erected a chaste and beautiful monument over his grave.

[NOTE 18.]

REV. BAXTER DICKINSON, D. D.

Born at Amherst, Massachusetts, April 14, 1795. His parents were Azariah Dickinson (a great-grandson of Nehemiah, fourth son of Nathaniel), and Mary, daughter of Joseph Eastman, of Amherst. Graduated at Yale, 1817; valedictorian at Andover, 1821; pastor of the Congregationalist Church, Longmeadow, Massssachusetts, 1823-1829; of Third Presbyterian Church, Newark, N. J., 1829-1835; Professor of Sacred Rhetoric and Pastoral Theology, Lane Theological Seminary, Cincinnati, Ohio, 1835-1839; and in Auburn Theological Seminary, New York, 1839-1847; Secretary of American and Foreign

Christian Union at Boston, Massachusetts; 1859-1868 in charge with his daughters of a successful seminary for young ladies, in Lake Forest, Indiana. The closing years of his life were spent in Brooklyn, New York, where he died December 7, 1875.

Dr. Dickinson was prominent in the temperance movement, and his "Alarm to Distillers," a prize essay, published by the Tract Society, was widely circulated. He was author of "Letters to Students," republished in England, and published many sermons.

In 1839 he was chosen Second Moderator of the New School General Assembly. The most remarkable production of his pen was "The True Doctrines," embodied in the protest of the minority against the exscinding acts of the General Assembly of 1837. This document was subsequently adopted by the famous Auburn Convention, and thence known as the Auburn Declaration. It was accepted by the two Presbyterian Churches when they again became one, as the symbol of their doctrinal harmony.

Dr. Dickinson was revered for learning, loyalty to the truth, Christian moderation and sound judgment. As a preacher he depended for effect more on the truth than on the arts of the orator. He filled with marked ability the responsible positions held by him.

Dr. Dickinson married, June 4, 1823, Martha, daughter of Jotham Bush, of Boylston, Massachuetts. Nine sons and daughters were born. The first, Richard Salter Storrs, was a Presbyterian clergyman of rare promise, who died in Edinburgh, Scotland, at thirty-two. William Cowper is also an honored minister in Indiana. Mary Taylor, Harriet Austin and Isabella Halstead are the surviving daughters.

[Note 19.]

GENERAL PHILEMON DICKINSON.

Philemon Dickinson was born at Croise-dore, Talbot County, Maryland, April 15, 1739. He was the son of Judge Samuel Dickinson and Mary Cadwalader, and youngest brother of Governor John Dickinson. He graduated at the University of Pennsylvania in 1757; was signer "Non Importation Resolutions," November 7, 1765; Colonel First New Jersey Militia, August to October, 1775; Brigadier-General, October, 1775, to June, 1777; Major-General, June, 1777, to October, 1781; Member New Jersey Provincial Convention, June, 1776; Chief Commissioner, Loan Office, New Jersey, 1781 to 1782; Member Continental Congress, 1782 to 1783; Vice-President New Jersey State Council, 1783 to 1785; Capital Commissioner, 1784; United States Senator, 1790 to 1793. He died February 4, 1809.

General Philemon Dickinson was distinguished for his zeal in the cause of his country, and for the very important services which he rendered in his military capacity at different stages of the war, and afterwards as a Senator of the United States.

When the main army took up its quarters at Morristown, after the battle of Princeton, General Dickinson was stationed on the west shore of the Millstone river, one of the nearest posts to the enemy, and there repelled a force. Washington says of this affair: "General Dickinson's behavior reflects the highest credit on him, for, though his troops were all new, he led them through the river middle deep under a severe fire, and gave the enemy so severe a charge that, although supported by three field pieces, they gave way, left their convoy and fled."

John Hancock, President of Congress, wrote to Governor Livingston, of New York, requesting in the name of Congress, that he would appoint General Dickinson to command the militia, and expressed confidence in his abilities and devotedness to the cause.

[Note 20.]

Letter from Daniel Webster.

"WASHINGTON, September 27, '50.

"MY DEAR SIR:—Our companionship in the Senate is dissolved. After this long and important session you are about to return to your home, and I shall try to find leisure to visit mine. I hope we may meet each other again, two months hence, for the discharge of our duties, in our respective stations in the Government. But life is uncertain, and I have not felt willing to take leave of you without placing in your hands a note, containing a few words which I wish to say to you.

"In the early part of our acquaintance, my dear sir, occurrences took place which I remember with constantly increasing regret and pain; because, the more I have known of you, the greater have been my esteem for your character and my respect for your talents. But it is your noble, able, manly and patriotic conduct in support of the great measures of this session, which has entirely won my heart and secured my highest regard. I hope you may live long to serve your country, but I do not think you are ever likely to see a crisis in which you may be able to do so much, either for your own distinction or for the public good. You have stood where others have fallen; you have advanced with firm and manly step where others have wavered, faltered and fallen back, and for one I desire to thank you and to commend your conduct out of the fulness of an honest heart.

"This letter needs no reply; it is, I am aware, of very little value, but I have thought you might be willing to receive it and, perhaps, to leave it where it would be seen by those who shall come after you.

"I pray you, when you reach your own threshold, to remember me most kindly to your wife and daughter, and I remain, my dear sir, with the truest esteem,

"Your Friend and Obt. Servt.,

"DANL. WEBSTER.

"HON. DANL. S. DICKINSON,
"U. S. Senate."

[NOTE 21.]

DR. EDMUND DICKENSON.

Edmund, the eldest son of Rev. William Dickenson, of Appleton, was born, 1624, at Appleton; died in London, 1707, leaving by his wife, Elizabeth Laddington, an only daughter, Elizabeth, who was married, first, to Sir G. Shires, second to Baron Blomberg. He was Fellow of the Royal College of Surgeons, President of Westminister Chemical School, Court Physician to Charles II. and James II., an intimate friend of the great French chemist, Theodore Mandamus, author of several medical and scientific works, in one of which he undertook to prove that the writings of Moses were confirmed by the Oracles of Apollo, at Delphi.

[NOTE 22.]

ANSON DICKINSON.

Anson, a descendant of Moses Dickinson, and the first of ten children of Oliver and Anna Landon Dickinson, was born at the home of his parents, in Milton, Litchfield

County, Connecticut, April 19, 1779. He died March 9, 1852, in his native village. He began painting early in life, and soon attained a remarkable skill in expressing the human face in minature.

In 1804 young Dickinson sat for his likeness to Malbone, in New York, and from observing his manner derived new stimulus and instruction. One of the sittings occurred on the day of the funeral of Alexander Hamilton, and the procession passed the window of Malbone's room. So absorbed was he in the business in hand that he neither paused himself to view the pageant, nor suffered his sitter to do so.

While yet young the artist was furnished with a letter of introduction to Gilbert Stuart, then at the head of American artists. Mr. Stuart said he had long wished to make his acquaintance. He had frequently seen his *paintings;* it was his wish to see him *paint;* and pointing to a portrait, he said: "The lady whose likeness that is, once complimented me in poetry, and I, her in painting. I wish you to make a copy in miniature, and to do it here, that I may see *how* you work." After a few days the picture was completed, to Mr. Stuart's entire satisfaction. "Now, my son," said he, "notwithstanding I have thus far invariably refused the numerous solicitations which have been made for my likeness, it will give me great pleasure to sit to you."

After his removal to New York, Anson Dickinson was for many years the first minature painter in the city. His house was the frequent resort of artists and amateurs of distinction. Stuart, Vanderlyn, Waldo, Fraser, etc. He was earnestly solicited to accept the Presidency of the Academy of Fine Arts, but his aversion to notoriety and public responsibility prompted him to decline. He was characterized by singular absence of self-assertion, preferring always to be sought for than to seek advantage. He was of fine personal presence and bearing, attracting attention wherever he was seen. His works were widely scattered throughout the country and brought him both money and fame. He painted miniatures of most of the noted men of his day; among them, Archbishop DuBois, Governor Oliver Wolcott, of Connecticut; Chancellor Livingston, of New York; the Seymours of Litchfield; Hon. Samuel Houston, of Texas.

One of his most celebrated pictures is his "Washington, at the age of forty," copied from Peale's original and engraved by J. W. Steel. It is now in the possession of Mr. A. Hoyt, of Stamford, Connecticut.

Among his works of imagination were, "The Graces," in possession of his adopted daughter, Mrs. Hon. Truman Smith, of Stamford, Connecticut; "Innocence" and "Hope," mentioned by Irving. His drawing and coloring were regarded by the best critics as perfect, and his miniatures retain the warmth and freshness of their first production. He excelled in portraying the female figure; nothing purer or more delicate than some of his sketches from fancy can be conceived. Like most eminent men, he had his detractors, but his name will outlast them all.

[NOTE 23.]

Letter from Washington Irving to Mrs. Hoffman, in New York, Dated

"JOHNSTOWN, N. Y., February 12, 1810.

"I was much interested and pleased while at Albany, with Dickinson, a young artist, who has resided there for some time past. He is an artist of highly promising talents, and of most amiable demeanor and engaging manners. I have endeavored to persuade him to leave this city of darkness and dullness and come to New York, and am strongly in hopes he will soon do so. He is not a mere mechanic in his art, but paints from his imagina-

tion. He has lately executed a figure of Hope, which does great credit to his invention and execution and bespeaks a most delicate and classic taste. He has promised to let me have it for a while to show it in New York. How I would glory in being a man of opulence, to take such young artists by the hand and cherish their budding genius. A few acts of munificence of the kind, done in a generous and liberal manner by some of our wealthy nabobs, would, I am satisfied, be more pleasing in the sight of Heaven, and more to the glory and advantage of this country than building a dozen shingle church steeples or buying a thousand venal votes at an election."
—Life of Irving, by Pierre M. Irving, Vol. I., Chap. XV.

[NOTE 24. BY REV. C. A. D.]

THE CHILDREN.

BY CHARLES M. DICKINSON.

When the lessons and tasks are all ended,
   And the school for the day is dismissed,
The little ones gather around me,
   To bid me good-night, and be kissed;
Oh, the little white arms that encircle
   My neck in their tender embrace!
Oh, the smiles that are halos of heaven,
   Shedding sunshine of love on my face!

And when they are gone I sit dreaming
   Of my childhood too lovely to last;
Of joy that my heart will remember,
   While it wakes to the pulse of the past,

Ere the world and its wickedness made me
  A partner of sorrow and sin,
When the glory of God was about me,
  And the glory of gladness within.

All my heart grows as weak as a woman's,
  And the fountains of feeling will flow,
When I think of the paths steep and stony,
  Where the feet of the dear ones must go,—
Of the mountains of Sin hanging o'er them,
  Of the tempests of Fate blowing wild ;
Ah, there's nothing on earth half so holy
  As the innocent heart of a child !

They are idols of hearts and of households ;
  They are angels of God in disguise ;
His sunlight still sleeps in their tresses,
  His glory still gleams in their eyes ;
Those truants from home and from heaven—
  They have made me more manly and mild ;
And I know now how Jesus could liken
  The kingdom of God to a child !

I ask not a life for the dear ones,
  All radiant, as others have done,
But that life may have just enough shadow
  To temper the glare of the sun ;
I would pray God to guard them from evil,
  But my prayer would bound back to myself ;
Ah ! a seraph may pray for a sinner,
  But a sinner must pray for himself.

The twig is so easily bended,
  I have banished the rule and the rod ;
I have taught them the goodness of knowledge,
  They have taught me the goodness of God.

My heart is the dungeon of darkness,
　Where I shut them for breaking a rule;
My frown is sufficient correction;
　My love is the law of the school.

I shall leave the old house in the Autumn,
　To traverse its threshold no more;
Ah! how I shall sigh for the dear ones,
　That meet me each morn at the door!
I shall miss the "good-nights" and the kisses,
　And the gush of their innocent glee,
The group on the green, and the flowers
　That are brought every morning for me.

I shall miss them at morn and at even,
　Their song in the school and the street;
I shall miss the low hum of their voices,
　And the tread of their delicate feet.
When the lessons of life are all ended,
　And death says, "The school is dismissed!"
May the little ones gather around me,
　To bid me good-night and be kissed.

This poem has often been accredited to Charles Dickens. The following bit of history, from "Waifs and Their Authors," (D. Lothrop & Co., Boston, Publishers,) explains the probable origin of the error:

DICKENS wrote many beautiful things, in that poetical prose into which he so often dropped, but he could never have written this any more than we could have penned "Pickwick." When he attempted verse—as we believe he rarely did—he made very unsatisfactory work of it. Certain minds think in rythm, as it were by instinct; and one of these gave us "The Children," but it was not the mind of "Boz." There are passages in some of DICKENS' stories which can be readily shaped into tolerable blank verse, but as blank verse, they would lose in effect, and DICKENS himself would have failed miserably in trying to shape them in it at the outset.

"The Children" was written by a partial namesake of the great story-teller—CHARLES M. DICKINSON—Some careless compositor may have been originally responsibile for the mistaken credit, owing to the similarity of names, as Mr. DICKINSON formerly wrote his without the "middle letter." When the sweet poem was penned—which was in the early summer of 1863—its author was a schoolmaster at Haverstraw, on the Hudson. He had to meet the almost universal dislike of scholars to writing compositions, and he chose a happy way of meeting it, by proposing to write something himself, to read on a Saturday afternoon, if they would do the same. The proposal made and accepted, the teacher's part on the programme must be filled, and hence we have "The Children," written after school was dismissed on Friday afternoon, and before it opened on the following morning. It was sent to a Boston paper, for which Mr. D. was then writing, and thereafter it went the rounds.

This is the simple story of a poem so simply, tenderly beautiful, that it has been printed over and over again in every paper in the land, has been extensively copied in Europe, and has won the heart of every true teacher, as it has won the admiration of all readers, by its delicate appreciation of youthful possibilities, its close sympathy with childhood, its warm love for childish ways. Simple as the poem is, it holds a rare sum of sweet philosophy within it. Indeed, the mystery of part of CHRIST's teachings seems to clarify in these lines :

> Those truants from home and from heaven,
> They have made me more manly and mild ;
> *And I know now how* JESUS *could liken*
> *The Kingdom of* GOD *to a child !*

Love of children is one of the purest elements in human nature, and it fairly glows in the whole poem. It is easy to see that the sympathetic teacher wrote it from the fullness of his heart,—wrote it perhaps, in the school-room itself, whence childish forms had hardly vanished, where the ring of childish voices had hardly died away, and with every token of childish presence, fresh and impressive.

[NOTE 25, BY REV. C. A. D.]

HYMN TO THE TRINITY.

BY LEIGH RICHMOND DICKINSON.

I.

Father of Lights ! from Thee my soul
  Beams forth, as Morning's early ray ;
Thy kindling life and glory roll,
  A radiant tide, along my day.

II.

O Son of God! Thy quenchless love
   Unfolds my heart, as Noon the flower;
Thy warmth, Thy beauty melt and move
   My cold life-stream with heavenly power.

III.

O Holy Ghost! like Evening dews
   Thy gracious consolations come;
Grateful as Evening's angel hues,
   That welcome weary pilgrims home

IV.

O sacred Three! O complete One!
   My Morn, my Noon, my Evening, blend
My life in perfect day, and crown
   This day with days that never end.

Of this hymn, the late Dr. William A. Muhlenberg, author of, "I would not live alway," and other poems, wrote the author: "Will you let me thank you for your exquisite hymn. It is worthy of Keble."

[NOTE 26.]

The Field family, to whom reference is here made, is not excelled in remarkable intellectual traits by any family this country has produced. Each of the children has risen to eminence in different fields, showing breadth of intellect and diversity of talent that amount to absolute genius. As their father did not display unusual ability, it is not unfair to assume that the remarkable traits these sons have shown, were largely inherited from their energetic and strong minded Dickinson mother.

ADDITIONAL NOTES.

Hon. Edward Dickinson.

Edward, first of Samuel Fowler and Lucretia Dickinson's nine children, was born on New Year's Day, 1803. He was educated in the public schools and in the academy of Amherst, and after entering the junior class of Amherst College, graduated, at twenty years of age, with the highest honors, at Yale. His law studies were under his father, and at the law school in Northampton. In 1826 he began practicing law in Amherst, and continued in it with large success until his death.

Edward Dickinson married (1), May 6, 1828, Emily, daughter of Joel and Betsey Norcross, of Monson, Massachusetts; after her death (2), Miss Vaill.

In 1838, '39 and '74 he was elected to the Legislature; in 1842 and '46 he was chosen senator; in 1845 and '46 one of the Governor's Council. From 1853 to 1855 he was a Member of Congress from Hampden and Hampshire counties.

In 1835 he was made Treasurer of Amherst College, and for thirty-nine years conducted its fiscal affairs with such advantage and exactness, that no error was found in his accounts.

Always above reproach in business, mindful of his obligations to others, he became an earnest Christian in 1850. His attendance was constant, his conduct in worship devout, his efforts in support of right redoubled. His pocket-book felt the new impulse. There was no worthy object to which his heart and his hand were not open.

His public spirit was proverbial. For the honor and prosperity of his native town, he wrought with energy and determination. Amherst owes her railroad advantages largely to his perseverance and foresight.

In 1874 he consented, with reluctance, to represent the interests of his district in the Legislature. After an exhausting speech in the House on the Massachusetts Central Railroad question, an almost instantaneous attack of paralysis overcame him, and he passed away in a few hours, on June 16, 1874.

In dignity, strength, and integrity of character, in professional and administrative ability and success, he was *primus inter pares*. His name stands eminent among Amherst's citizens, an illustrious example of Christian manhood.

NATHAN DICKINSON.

Nathan Dickinson, mentioned in the introduction, was born in Amherst, Massachusetts, in 1799. He was a business man of great energy and ability. He removed to Michigan in 1840, and accumulated a large property. He was a man of decision and of generous impulses. He promoted education and objects of philanthropic and material progress. He died in 1861. His family now reside in Westfield, Massachusetts.

77 WALL STREET,
NEW HAVEN, Conn., August 24, 1883.

Mr. F. W. Dickinson:

DEAR SIR—I am just in receipt of a letter from my friend and townsman, M. F. Dickinson, jr., Esq., of Boston, expressing regret that in the bustle of your family gathering at Amherst he neglected to announce that I had for sale a few of the Hadley genealogies.

Mr. Dickinson suggests that I ask you to notice the above book in the printed volume of your family proceedings. You are probably aware that Judd's History of Hadley has been out of print at least fifteen (15) years.

I presume that nowhere else so full an account is found in print of the descendants of your ancestor, Nathaniel Dickinson, of Wethersfield and Hadley. The records there given will stimulate inquiry into the genealogy of the family of Dickinson, whose genealogy ought surely to be printed in separate form.

     I remain, Yours Truly,
        LUCIUS M. BOLTWOOD.

A few copies of the genealogical portion of Judd's History of Hadley, Massachusetts, embracing descendants of Nathaniel Dickinson, the first settler, and allied families, a closely printed octavo of 168 pages, will be sent to any address for $2.00, by the compiler, Lucius M. Boltwood, 77 Wall Street, New Haven, Connecticut.

PROPOSED FAMILY HISTORY.

The undersigned were appointed an Historical Committee, with the view of gathering materials, which might form a more complete and satisfactory history of the family. To this end, Wharton Dickinson, Esq., of the Committee, has prepared at our request, the following

PROSPECTUS.

Genealogy is a subject which we Americans, in our haste to get rich, have sadly neglected ; it has too often been coupled with the word aristocracy, a term which was brought into very general disrepute in America during the struggle between Great Britain and the Colonies ; and justly so, for unfortunately, the majority of the English nobility were at that time leagued against us. Another cause of disfavor was the fact that the ranks of the Tories in this country, were largely recruited from the then Colonial aristocracy. Thank God, there were noble exceptions to this rule. The Schuylers, Livingstons, Jays, Van Cortlands and Morrises, of New York ; the Daytons, Stocktons, Scuddens, Odgens and Freylinghuysens, of New Jersey ; the Cadwalladers, Clymers, Biddles, Merediths and Mifflins, of Pennsylvania ; the Reeds and Bayards, of Delaware ; the Carrols and Howards, of Maryland ; the Lees, Washingtons and Randolphs, of Virginia, and the Middletons, Pinckneys and Rutledges, of South Carolina, formed a noble band of patriots, who expended freely of their blood and treasures, that America might be free. But unfortunately the larger number of the Colonial aristocracy sided with Britain; hence, as we before observed, the word aristocracy fell into general disrepute, and those families who formerly bore arms by right of birth, very generally discarded their use, and as every one had his or her part to perform in the future development of a great nation, there was little, if any, time left to trace out families or lineage.

But now we have finished the first century of our existence as a nation, and have fairly entered upon the second; and we also begin to look back with pleasure upon the records made by our sires in the days of '76, and also in the early settlement of the country. Family reunions are now beginning to be held in every section of the country, and those of the same race, from Maine to California, and from the Lakes to the Gulf, gather together, at the old homes of their ancestors, and in addresses and poems recount the trials and triumphs of the founders of this great country. There is also a growing desire to know more of the history of the various branches of the parent tree, and for this purpose historical and genealogical works are now being published in many quarters, not with the purpose of fostering self-love and false pride, but to show what *has* been done in the past, what is now *being* done, and what *must* be done in the future. We may not all be statesmen or generals, but each, in his own individual sphere, has a duty to perform to a common country, and in the cause of Christ and humanity, and nothing can be more stimulating to us all than to recount the deeds of our sires.

Probably no family in America played a more prominent part in the struggle for Independence than that of Dickinson. The names of John Dickinson, the "Farmer of Pennsylvania;" Gen. Philemon Dickinson, of New Jersey; Col. Henry Dickinson, of Maryland; Major Nathaniel Dickinson, of Virginia, and his brothers, Richard and Elijah, and Henry Dickinson, of Russel

County, Virginia; Reuben Dickinson, of Amherst, Massachusetts; Oliver, of Milton, Connecticut, and others, deserve to be enrolled among the great worthies of their country. Nor have their descendants proved themselves unworthy of their illustrious descent: instance, Daniel S. Dickinson, Samuel Fowler Dickinson, Mahlon and Philemon Dickerson, and others. It is for the purpose of recounting the history of this family, from the earliest to the latest times, that this work has been undertaken, and it is to be hoped that it will not only be the means of drawing us nearer by the kindred ties of blood, but that we may be stimulated to renewed exertions, and that our successors may ever keep fresh and unstained, the family honor and the family escutcheon, and above all, keeping ever in mind our family motto: "*Esse Quam Videri,*" to *be* rather than to appear.

All histories, whether of nations or races, are composed partly of tradition and partly of fact; that of the Dickinsons is no exception to the rule. Part First will be divided into two chapters; the first treating of the traditionary history of the race; the second, the actual history of the family in England. Part Second will treat of the descendants of Charles Dickinson, of London; Part Third, of the descendants of Thomas, of Ayrshire; Part Fourth, of the descendants of Deacon Nathaniel Dickinson; Part Fifth, those of Philemon Dickerson. The Index will contain all names in the female line, and others connected with the history of the race.

In order to facilitate this work, the undersigned request answers to the following questions:

First—Who are your ancestors in the Dickinson line, as far back as you can trace them? Be particular to give the date and place of birth; date and place of marriage, and to whom; date and place of death.

Second—What were the names of the children of your direct male ancestors, as far as you know, and whom did they marry, and when and where, and who are the proper persons to address to obtain information concerning *them?*

Third—What profession or occupation did your said male ancestors follow? What civil, military or naval offices did they fill (if any), either national, state, county or municipal, and where, and during what period; and if college graduates, at *what* college?

Fourth—If they have been college presidents or professors, deacons or elders, or church wardens, please state in what place and during what period; also, same information regarding secret societies?

Fifth—When were you born; when were you married, where, and to whom; what issue have you had. Are any married, and if so, to whom, and what issue have *they?* Also, please answer questions three and four, regarding yourself and your posterity. The same information is desired of husbands of female descendants.

Affectionately, Your Kinsmen,

REV. CHARLES A. DICKINSON,
WHARTON DICKINSON,
MAHLON H. DICKINSON,
REV. LEGH R. DICKINSON,
CHARLES M. DICKINSON,
Historical Committee.

TRADITION.

[*The following chapter will serve as a specimen of the work proposed.*]

In the year 776, there appeared at the Court of Halfdan Huilbein, King of Norway, a soldier of fortune, named Ivar, a native of the Uplands. Burke, in his Extinct Peerage, article "Sinclair," says, he was of noble birth, and a direct descendant of the dignified hero, Thor. Prof. Philip H. Dunham, of the University of Oxford, in his "History of Scandinavia," says, he was originally a shepherd, and followed his flocks and herds up the craggy and ice-bound sides of the Snashattan, a snow-crowned peak, which lifts its mighty head 8,000 feet above the sea. One day, as he fed his flocks on the lowlands, a roving band of Northmen, struck by his great height and apparent physical strength, captured him and took him off to sea. Here he followed an adventurous life for many years, during which, it is said, he visited the coasts of Iceland and Greenland, and even reached the coasts of New England—a country peopled by descendants of his, nearly a thousand years later. Be this as it may, just a thousand years prior to the independence of America, Ivar suddenly reappeared in Norway, and presented himself at the Norse King's Court. Being of handsome presence and stalwart build, and, moreover, having achieved a reputation that made his name famous throughout Scandinavia, he was welcomed with open arms by the aged monarch, the last male descendant of the great Woden, that occupied the throne of Norway. Dissensions were continually taking place at Court; rival chiefs were aspiring to the crown; and the old king was filled with apprehension lest the crown of his ancestors should be wrested from him. He had but one child, a daughter, Eurittea, the darling of his old age; a maiden with blue eyes and golden locks—a striking contrast to the bent form and white locks of her aged sire. The appearance of Ivar at Court, however, soon changed the aspect of affairs. Halfdan commissioned him general of his army, and by his powerful aid, order was soon restored. But a still greater honor awaited this adventurous child of fortune. The lovely Eurittea was given to him in marriage, and the birth of their son Eystein, in 780, was made the occasion of great rejoicing throughout Norway. By a royal decree, the infant prince was made the successor of his venerable grandsire, who died about 790. Ivar became regent during his son's minority, who assumed the reins of power about A. D. 800. After a long and prosperous reign, during which he raised Norway to a height of prosperity never before attained, he died in 855, leaving issue, three sons that we know of.

First, Harold, his successor; second, Rogenwald, of whom hereafter; third, Malahule, ancestor of the great Norman house of De Tocni, hereditary standard bearers of Normandy, from a younger son of whom, who settled at Lindsai, County Essex, England, *temp.* William the Conqueror, springs the noble Scotch house of Lindsay, Earls of Crawford and Balcarras.

Rogenwald was born about the year 820. By his father he was created Earl of Maere and Raumdahl, in the Uplands, Norway. When his brother Harold Harfagr, succeeded to the throne of Norway, in 855, he became a firm supporter of that monarch, in his plans to subdue the independent chiefs of Norway, and was argely instrumental in establishing Harold as King of all Norway. He also led a large fleet against the Orkney and Shetland Islands, which he wrested from the dominion of the King of Scots, and by Harold was created Sovereign Earl of Orkney, in 888, and was founder of two powerful lines of princes, the elder of which ruled the Orkney and Shetland Isles for five centuries, frequently intermarrying with the royal line of Scotland; and the younger of which became Dukes of Normandy, and finally Kings of England. Rogenwald, or as Forsyth in his "Beauties of Scotland," calls him, Ronald, died at Rosslyn Castle, in the Orkneys, in 910. Forsyth says he was one hundred and thirty years old when he died, but the best authorities say he was ninety. His tomb was discovered during the latter part of the last century, while some repairs were being made in Rosslyn Chapel. He left issue, four sons.

First—Rogenwald, Earl of Maere and Ranmdahl, in the Uplands.

Second—Eynar, Second Earl of Orkney. His great-great-granddaughter Margaret, Countess Palatine, of Orkney, married Madoc, Earl of Athole, son of Earl Melmare, who was a younger son of King Duncan I., of Scotland, and brother of Malcolm Canmore, thus carrying the title to the royal line of Scotland.

Third—Manifred, who conquered Denmark, and was the great grandfather of Canute, King of Denmark and England.

Fourth—Rolf, of whom hereafter.

Rolf, or as he is more familiarly known, Rollo, was one of the most adventurous princes of his age. He was born about the year 850. At an early age he took command of a large fleet of ships and set out on a piratical cruise. He first made descents on the coasts of Scotland, but the sturdy Scotch soon sent him about his business. He next tried the eastern and southern coasts of England, with equal success. He then entered the mouth of the Scheldt and ravaged Friesland. But a more inviting field soon offered itself to his rapacious grasp. France was at that time groaning under the miserable rule of the imbecile successors of the great Charlemange. In 876 Charles Le Chauve (the Bald) was King of Neustria. His throne was beset by insurgent nobles and princes. Rollo soon became aware of this state of affairs, and in November, 876, he entered the mouth of the Seine, and soon conquered Rouen, which he made his headquarters, but Charles bought him off in 877. In 881 he again entered France and was defeated at Saucourt; but strange to say, the French became demoralized at the close of the day, and enabled Rollo to collect his scattered forces and retire in good order. He recaptured Rouen, July 25, 882, but retired before the close of the year to Norway.

In the fall of 885 he again entered France, and sailing up the Seine laid seige to Paris. The siege lasted from November 25, 885, to October, 886, when Charles bought Rollo off for £700 in silver. For the next three years Rollo assisted his father, Earl Rogenwald, in the subjugation of the Orkneys, but in 889 he once more visited France and overran Brittany, and once again was he bought off and retired. For the next fourteen years we lose sight of Rollo. He is said to have been one of those adventurous Northmen who visited the coasts of Newfoundland and New England, with Eric the Red, in 901-2. In 903 he again made his appearance in France and burnt Tours, but soon retired. In 911 he laid siege to Paris the second time. Charles le Simple (the Simple) was now king. His advisers saw the folly of treating with the fierce Northmen in the old way, and by their advice, Charles sent the Archbishop of Rouen to offer him the hand of his daughter Gisele in marriage, and all the country between the sea (English channel), the rivers Epte and Aure, and the frontiers of Marie and

Brittany. The meeting between Charles and Rollo took place at the town of St. Clair, on the Epte. Rollo complained that the country offered him was sterile. Charles offered him Brittany in addition, a very generous offer, considering the fact that Brittany did not belong to him. That was a very small matter to Rollo, however, who could win by the sword what he could not acquire by purchase.

When the Archbishop requested Rollo to kiss Charles in acknowledgement of the latter's sovereignty, the former exclaimed, Nese-bi-Gott! (No, by God) at which the French laughed and nicknamed the Normans bigoths Rollo ordered one of his followers to perform this office for him, but the churl did it so roughly, that the old King was thrown on his back amidst the jeers and laughter of his *loving* subjects.

Rollo was baptised by the Archbishop of Rouen in the feast of Epiphany, in January, 912, and received the Christian name of Robert, and at Easter was married to Gisele with great ceremony. To the astonishment of all Christendom this barbarian became one of the wisest and ablest princes in Europe. He died in 917, leaving, with possibly others:

First, William, Second Duke of Normandy; second, Geoffrey, Count of Rouen; third, Walter, Count of Caen.

Walter, Count of Caen, received a grant of the town and castle of Caen from his father Rollo, and from him is said to have sprung: Gaultier de Caen (Walter of Caen), one of the Norman companions of the Conqueror. Gaultier's name does not appear on any of the English rolls of the Conquerors, but is only to be found on the roll in the Church of Dives, Normandy, published in the latter part of the last century, by M. Leopold de Lisle, Member of the Institute at Paris. A copy of this book will be found in the Astor Library, New York. Gaultier is said to have received a grant of the Saxon Manor of

Kenson, on the Aire, in the West Riding of Yorkshire, but no such manor appears in Domesday's work, nor do we know anything further of Gaultier, than that he came over with William in 1066, and that a descendant of his was Clerk in Chancery, *temp.* Edward I. Blake, in his Biographical Dictionary of the Judges of England, says:

"John de Caen was Chief Clerk in Chancery from 1292 to 1302; he held the great seal as Chancellor, and in 1298 acted in Exchequer as *locum tenens* for the Chancellor. He was Receiver of Petitions to the Parliament of 1305-7, and that of 1310. He died in London in 1312, leaving issue."

The best authorities say that the name Dickenson either comes from the Manor of Kenson, in Yorkshire, or from the name of De Caen,—De Caen's son—and that Hugh Dikenson, or Dicconsin, who was living in or near Leeds, *temp.* Henry VI., was a descendant of John de Caen. Chapter Second, however, will trace the family back in England as far as it can be done, in a continuous line, from Charles of London, including all the branches that have come to America since 1620. There are many ways of spelling the name; we give them in the order of their antiquity:

De Caen (or by some De Kenson), Dikenson, Dicconsin, Dickenson, Dickinson, Dickerson, Dickonson, Dickeson, Dickison, and Dickason. This closes Chapter First, which is tradition only so far as relates to the connection between our race and the Northmen. The facts regarding Rollo and his sires being pretty well authenticated by history.

IN MEMORIAM.

Since the Reunion at Amherst, death has entered the family, and a number of those who were with us either in person or spirit have entered "the pale realms of shade." The aged have been taken, ripe in usefulness and honor, and two have been cut off in the very flower of beauty and promise. The committee having this publication in charge believe that the family will be interested in such brief biographical sketches of the recent dead as they have been able to obtain.

WM. L. DICKINSON.

William Leverett Dickinson, the first child of Cotton Gaylord and Lucy Stone Dickinson, was born in Windsor, Vermont, January 9, 1819. The family soon after removed to St. Johnsburg, Vermont. At thirteen he met with a painful accident, which deprived him of his right hand, and partially disabled his left. He entered Lynden Academy, and graduated at nineteen from the University of Vermont. Later he became principal of an academy for boys, in Jersey City, which he conducted for several years with marked success. August 28, 1843, he married Celia Goss, daughter of Philip Goss, of Lynden, Vermont. In 1861 he was admitted to the bar in New York; in 1867 was appointed Superintendent of Schools of Jersey City and Hudson County, which position he held until his death.

As an educator, Mr. Dickinson stood in the front rank. He magnified his office, and was faithful and conscientious in the discharge of his duties. His high moral and Christian character made his death a calamity. He was sensitively conscientious, and very decided in convictions, but of great kindliness and depth of sympathy. Himself alone he never excused, fulfilling to the letter all that his position demanded of him.

He was identified with all the principal benevolent enterprises of the city, Secretary of the Bible Society and City Missions, Treasurer of the Society for the Relief of Soldiers, during the Civil War, Bank Director, and an active member and officer of the First Reformed Church of Jersey City.

He died in Jersey City, November 3, 1883.

ANDREW DICKINSON.

Andrew Dickinson was born in Milton, Litchfield County, Connecticut, in January, 1801. He died December 12, 1883, at his home in Ridgewood, New Jersey. He was the last of the ten children of Oliver and Anna Dickinson, and the youngest brother of Anson and Daniel, the celebrated miniature painters. He married Elvira, daughter of David Catlin, of Milton, and had two children, Legh Richmond and Helen Catlin, the latter of whom died in 1868. He was a man of childlike simplicity and sterling integrity.

Mr. Dickinson was for twenty years connected with the Mercantile Agency of R. G. Dun & Co., New York. For seven or eight years he had been unable to work, but in recognition of his useful services the firm presented him with an annual pension.

Mr. Dickinson was also an author of merit, both in poetry and prose. A volume of descriptive and sacred poetry was commended and enjoyed by many lovers of genuine feeling and glowing fancy. Many of his hymns have been sung in Sunday schools, and are found in the Sunday school collections. One of them, "Jacob's Prayer," has been translated and sung in the Chinese language.

On his return, in 1850, from a voyage for health, to England, Scotland, Ireland, Wales and France, he published "My First Visit to Europe," which was very highly prized for its simplicity and purity of style.

JULIETTE DICKINSON.

Juliette Dickinson, wife of Linus Dickinson, of Springfield, Massachusetts, died February 10th, 1884, aged seventy-eight years. Her husband survives, and was present at the Amherst meeting. They had lived together over fifty years.

EMMA ALLGOOD DICKINSON.

Emma Allgood Dickinson, daughter of Francke W. and Katie May (Allgood) Dickinson, was born December 4th, 1873. She was a child of bright intellectual, and of marked moral, qualities. Truthfulness and conscientiousness adorned her conduct. She was a good scholar, in advance of many of her schoolmates. Though mature for her years, she was full of the joy and zest of childhood. She had a faculty of saying the right thing in the right place, and her apt reply, quoted in the Historical Address, is one of many illustrations of this gift. She died in Springfield, Massachusetts, February 19, 1884, and to no child are more appropriate the Master's words: "Of such is the Kingdom of Heaven."

May Dickinson.

May E. Dickinson, only daughter of Rev. Legh R. and Mary E. Dickinson, was born at Kingsbridge, Westchester County, New York, December 28th, 1860. From her earliest years she was a child of promise, wise, purehearted, genial and deeply loving. All who knew her admired and loved her. She had rare gifts of mind, and excelled in music, painting, poetry, correspondence and in conversation. Her wealth of heart was not less ample. Confirmed at eleven years, she always said that she was "the Saviour's very own." She graduated at St. Mary's, Burlington, New Jersey, in 1878, the youngest and the pet of her class, and one of the three first in honor. She entered into Life on Saturday evening, June 7, 1884, after passing through five months of suffering, saying to each of her parents, "Be cheerful," and to her brother, "Be a good boy," falling asleep after kissing each of her family and uttering the words, "It is all right." She died in the communion of the Church, and is with the angels in Paradise. She said on the last morning of her life here: "The angels are about me." She was buried in the cemetery of Grace Church, Great Bend, Pennsylvania, June 10, amid many tears of the people and the children, who lined her grave with evergreens and flowers. Her poems show rare purity of thought and tenderness of soul, which were the qualities of her character. The members of the Dickinson family will be glad to read the poem here presented, "for a memorial of her," and the tribute from the editor of the Binghamton *Republican*, published on the day of her burial.

[Binghamton Daily Republican, June 10, 1884.]

DEATH IN JUNE.

"She thought our good-night kiss was given,
 And like a lily her life did close;
 Angels uncurtained that repose,
And the next dawning was in heaven."

It is June again, but not June everywhere. Into some hearts December has entered, though "December's not pleasant as *May*." June sunshine weaves its golden woof about the world, but the background is black as night. June's bird songs are in the air, but the gamut is broken and music is out of tune and time. June flowers embalm the earth with sweetness, but they merely offer up their lives in token of the fragrant life that has left the world. In the midst of all the joyous and exuberant life now bursting from sod, bush, nest and tree, Death rudely enters to remind us he claims all seasons for his own.

On Saturday last, Miss May, only daughter of Rev. L. R. and Mary E. Dickinson, of Great Bend, passed from life unto Life. For months she had maintained the desperate and unequal struggle, but one by one the vital forces were wasted, and at last, after many periods of hope and partial recovery, Death triumphed.

The deceased was a young lady of rare endowments and accomplishments, and of sweet and beautiful disposition and spirit. Only a short time before her illness she visited friends in this city, and impressed every one who met her with her buoyant life, her amiable character, most engaging manners and rare intelligence. Among her other accomplishments she contributed to several leading periodicals, and some of her contributions possessed unusual merit and indications of brilliant promise. In the wide sympathy felt for her bereaved family we beg to very tenderly and earnestly join.

IN MEMORIAM.

THE GOLDEN GATE OF CHILDHOOD.

BY MAY DICKINSON.

Among Life's melodies to which we listen,
  What one so sweet,
As the soft ripple of the childish laughter,—
  The pattering feet?

Oh, happy days of childhood, with their sunshine
  Undimmed by care!
Oh, little, trusting hearts, with fond illusions
  So real, so fair!

But toward the gate the steps are ever tending,
  Nearer they go;
Wide on its hinges swings the fairy fretwork,
  Noiseless and slow.

And out on Life's broad highway troop the children,
  Strong in their youth,
Bravely they start on their long journey, seeking
  Love, honor, truth.

Onward they go, yet oft they turn, and, wistful,
  Lingeringly wait
To catch bright glimpses through the gold-barred portals
  Of that closed gate.

The gentle hand that shut it fast forever,
  They cannot see;
But a low voice through their young souls, deep thrilling,
  Speaks lovingly:

"Peace! Keep thy child-heart strong, and true and tender,
  Whate'er thy fate;
So shall the years bring glimpses of thy childhood
  Through the closed gate.

"Glimpses that are foretokenings and revealings
  Of the bright door
Of a new youth, perpetual and immortal,
  Closing no more."

www.ingramcontent.com/pod-product-compliance
Lightning Source LLC
Chambersburg PA
CBHW031816230426
43669CB00009B/1167